REFORMATION
SKETCHES

REFORMATION
SKETCHES

INSIGHTS INTO
LUTHER, CALVIN, AND
THE CONFESSIONS

W. ROBERT GODFREY

PUBLISHING
P.O. BOX 817 • PHILLIPSBURG • NEW JERSEY 08865

Chapters 1–17 appeared originally in *The Outlook* and are reprinted here by permission. *Chap. 1:* 44 (Nov. 1994): 8–11; (Dec. 1994): 16–17; 45 (Jan. 1995): 19–21. *Chap. 2:* 41 (June 1991): 22–23. *Chap. 3:* 42 (Jan. 1992): 19. *Chap. 4:* 42 (Oct. 1992): 15–16. *Chap. 5:* 46 (Dec. 1996): 18–19. *Chap. 6:* 40 (Oct. 1990): 16. *Chap. 7:* 48 (Jan. 1998): 17–19. *Chap. 8:* 41 (Oct. 1991): 5–6. *Chap. 9:* 42 (July 1992): 20. *Chap. 10:* 43 (Feb. 1993): 29–31. *Chap. 11:* 51 (Feb. 2001): 18–19; (Mar. 2001): 20–22. *Chap. 12:* 40 (Mar. 1990): 24–25. *Chap. 13:* 48 (Dec. 1998): 14–15. *Chap. 14:* 49 (Mar. 1999): 22–24. *Chap. 15:* 45 (Apr. 1995): 7–8. *Chap. 16:* 26 (June 1976): 18–21. *Chap. 17:* 46 (Feb. 1996): 15–17.

Permission to use illustrations 1 and 2 has been granted by Mary Ann Jeffreys Archives; 3 and 6 by the Pitts Theology Library, Candler School of Theology, Emory University; 4 and 5 by the Meeter Center, Hekman Library, Calvin.

Page design and typesetting by Lakeside Design Plus

Printed in the United States of America

Library of Congress Cataloging-in-Publication Data

Godfrey, W. Robert
    Reformation Sketches : insights into Luther, Calvin, and the confessions / W. Robert Godfrey.
        p. cm.
Includes bibliographical references (p.) and index
ISBN 0-87552-578-4
1. Reformation. 2. Luther, Martin, 1483–1546. 3. Calvin, Jean, 1509–1564. 4. Reformed Church—Creeds—History and criticism. I. Title

BR315.G63 2003
270.6—dc21

2002045042

To Mary Ellen
who never hindered my work,
but as fellow historian always encouraged
and enhanced it.

CONTENTS

CONTENTS

ILLUSTRATIONS

ACKNOWLEDGMENTS

As I reflect on my indebtedness to many people, I would express my thanks first to my parents, Bill and Alice Godfrey, who always encouraged me in my curious desire to study history. I want to thank my teachers in history, particularly Dr. Lewis Spitz, Dr. Wilhelm Pauck, and Dr. Heiko Oberman, with whom I studied at Stanford University, and Dr. Philip Edgcumbe Hughes and Dr. Roger Nicole, with whom I studied at Gordon-Conwell Theological Seminary. I thank my colleagues at Westminster Theological Seminary in Philadelphia and Westminster Theological Seminary in California, Escondido, for encouragement and stimulation. I thank Tom and Laurie Vanden Heuvel, dear friends, who served as editors of *The Outlook*, where these essays first were published. Especially I would thank Mary Ellen, who always thought this book would have to be dedicated to my first wife, who died by degrees. Mary Ellen helped immeasurably in clarifying my thoughts and straightening out my prose.

INTRODUCTION

All historians would agree that the great Reformation of the sixteenth century was one of the most important events in the history of the church. Its impact on the unity of the church is rivaled only by the division between eastern Orthodoxy and western Roman Catholicism in 1054. Its impact on the doctrine and life of the church can be compared with the dramatic impact of the fourth century—a century that witnessed a fundamental change in the relations between church and state with the conversion of the emperor Constantine, a clear statement on the divinity of Jesus at the Council of Nicea, and the foundations of Augustine's doctrine of grace. The influence of the Reformation has unquestionably been the dominant force in Protestantism for centuries.

Today, however, some people seem to believe that the Protestant churches have moved away from the Reformation as their defining experience. Liberalism, evangelicalism, Pentecostalism, ecumenism, and postmodernism are post-Reformation phenomena that shape contemporary church life more than the Reformation. Many seem to think that the Reformation is old news: get over it.

The sketches in this book strive to show that the Reformation remains vitally important for Christians today. First, this book looks at some of the great leaders of the Reformation, both those who are still famous (Luther and Calvin) and those who have been largely forgotten (Melanchthon and Vermigli). While it is fashionable among many professional historians to disparage the role of great men in history, I remain convinced that God does raise up uniquely gifted leaders for his church in distinct periods of history. Their role and influence are critical to God's providential governing of his people. The Reformers and preachers of the sixteenth century were the best educated, most godly, and most faithful group of leaders the church has ever seen. In a remarkable way they combined commitment, learning, and orthodoxy. We need to continue to learn from them.

Second, these sketches look at the role of some of the Reformed confessions in the life of the church. The confessions powerfully summarize for us the wisdom and biblical learning of that age which must continue to help and instruct us today. The insight of another era is invaluable as it helps to rescue us from the parochialism of the present.

Third, these essays remind us of how important the institution of the church was for the Reformers. They reformed not only doctrine and individuals but also the church and its practices. They helped the people of God to live in ways that conformed more closely to biblical teaching than they had done in the past. The Reformers' care for the church needs to inform and inspire us today.

Finally, these brief studies remind us that the Reformers' primary concern was to preach and teach the gospel. They did that passionately and clearly. Their witness to the gospel is needed as much in the twenty-first century as at any other time. The confusion about the basic meaning of the gospel even in Protestant circles is astounding and frightening. Reading about the Reformers will humble us as we see that they already anticipated nearly all of the religious questions that we are debating today. Their words echo down the centuries to help us understand the Scriptures' teaching on the work of Christ and to lead us to faith in him.

- Reformation is recognized as import today
- Reformed confessions influence us
- Church was impt to reformers
- concern to preach truth gospel

PART ONE

Luther

AND THE REFORMATION

1

LUTHER ON
LAW AND GOSPEL

round October 31, Martin Luther is remembered far and wide in the United States among evangelical Protestants as a hero of the faith. We look back at Luther as a pioneer, as a profound theologian, as a heroic reformer. Some of us gather in Reformation Day services on October 31st to remember the great beginning of the Reformation.

On other days of the year, however, we Reformed Christians are often inclined to harbor at least some suspicions about Martin Luther. Is it true that Martin Luther did not fully reform the church from Roman Catholic elements? We may think particularly about sacraments and ceremonies as areas in which Luther may not have done all that he should have done. We may also suspect that Luther had a bit of an

disciple or adherent

antinomian tendency. Does his stress on the distinction between the law and the gospel go too far? Did Luther make too little of the law? We as Reformed Christians may fear that he has tipped the balance on the side of antinomianism. We may harbor such suspicions about Luther because the Lutherans constantly harbor suspicions that we have tipped the balance in the direction of moralism.

LUTHER'S STYLE

Since Lutherans and Reformed people tend to enjoy trading insults with one another—we accusing them of being monophysites and they accusing us of being Nestorians, for example—it is appropriate that we take a look again at Martin Luther and ask ourselves, What did Luther really say about the law and the gospel? What can we learn from him, and are there any areas in which we may have legitimate concern? It is not always easy for us as Reformed Christians to read Martin Luther. We need to realize that if we are going to read him—and we should because there is great spiritual profit in reading Martin Luther—that Martin Luther sometimes uses words with different definitions from the ones we are accustomed to using. Particularly in his use of the words *law* and *gospel*, we will see that he does tend to define them differently from the way in which Reformed folk define them.

We also need to bear in mind that Luther's style is rather different from the style of most Reformed authors. Luther was an expert in the use of hyperbole. Luther loved to exaggerate to make a point. And if we do not bear that in mind as we read Martin Luther, if we lift his statements out of context, we will surely misunderstand him. He loved to drive home a point by exaggeration. One of my favorite examples is when he once said, "All callings are honorable before God." He was resisting the medieval notion that only priests, monks, and nuns had a calling. He was insisting every Christian occupation is a calling. He said all callings are honorable before God "with the possible exceptions of burglary and prostitution." He was not promoting burglary and prostitution, but he was exaggerating to make a point.

Luther exaggerated in part because of his reaction to medieval theology. Luther said the most important word in medieval theology was the Latin word *ergo* ("therefore"). He said the besetting sin of Latin theology was "therefore"—constantly resting their theology on the conclusions of human reason. He said the real word that should be at the center of our theology is the German word *dennoch* ("nevertheless"). Theology operates not by therefores but by neverthelesses. We as Reformed theologians following that nice, balanced lawyer, John Calvin, may tend to be more sympathetic to therefores. But if we are going to understand Luther, we have to understand his use of the nevertheless to drive home his point. He exaggerates and at times overemphasizes.

This point is even more important when we remember that Luther was not in the strictest sense a systematic theologian. He was an occasional theologian. He never wrote a full systematic theology. He never even sat down to write his projected systematic treatise on justification. He wrote to specific issues in the life of the church. He exaggerated as he felt necessary for the occasion.

Also, he wrote at great speed. When he wrote his treatise in 1520, *The Babylonian Captivity of the Church*, which was his analysis of the sacraments of the church, he began the treatise saying that there were three sacraments: penance, baptism, and the Lord's Supper. He concluded the treatise saying there were two sacraments. He had developed his thought in the course of writing the treatise but had no time to go back and revise it. We need to bear this in mind as we read and study Martin Luther.

LUTHER'S LIFE

Let us begin by looking at Luther's life: Luther the radical conservative. Luther, I think, must be understood as a conservative who took conservative principles to a radical conclusion. Luther had nothing of the revolutionary in his soul. He did not seek to change the church. He did not set out to make all things new. He did not really like change. He reached his reforming conclusions by taking the conservative positions of the medieval church to their logical conclusions. He was a radical conservative. As Heiko Oberman argues in his biography, *Luther, Man Between God and the Devil*,[1] Luther was not really a reformer. He did not set out in any conscious or perhaps even unconscious sense to reform the church. There had been many reformers through the Middle Ages. Luther did not have anything of that sense about himself, Oberman argues. Luther was much more the prophet who comes to challenge the people that they have not lived up to their ideals. Luther comes to Protestant conclusions not so much out of a desire to change or out of a desire to be a revolutionary but out of a desire to get the church to be consistent with its own most basic principles.

Luther grew up living the traditional life as the son of a prospering German businessman. He grew up as a loyal and obedient son. His father looked around and asked what his son should do to advance the family fortunes. The answer in his day—as well as in ours—was to become a lawyer. So Papa Luther determined to send his son off to study the law. And loyal, faithful son Martin went to study law. Yet Luther went with a heavy heart because he was not only a loyal son of his family. He was also a loyal son of the church.

The church had been educating Luther with the truth that one must take care of one's soul. The church told Martin Luther that the soul is a precious thing and that the salvation of the soul was difficult to accomplish. The church advised that anyone who wanted to be serious about his soul and about salvation should become a monk because the life of a monk was precisely the life of giving oneself over to the salvation of one's soul. When Luther became a monk, he did so because he was a conservative. He had listened to the voice of the church that said to him, You need to take care of your soul first and foremost. He illustrated the medieval proverb that said doubt makes the monk. Luther became a monk because he doubted. He doubted his relationship to God.

Luther's very enthusiasm for monasticism made him in some ways obnoxious in the monastery. He kept going to his confessor to confess minor sins. The confessor kept sending him away, saying he did not want to talk to him because he did not have anything significant to confess. Yet Luther was burdened with a sense of his sin and tried to make faithful use of the medieval sacrament of penance to deal with his sin.

Luther's Studies

A wise leader in the monastery set Luther to work studying because he recognized him as a man of unusual brilliance. Luther began to study. Although this is something of an oversimplification, we can say his study led him to two critical theological conclusions: one in the area of authority and the other in the area of salvation.

The Matter of Authority

If we look first at the matter of authority, we see that the late medieval tradition was rather undifferentiated and somewhat confused in its approach to authority. The late medieval tradition said that the Bible was authority, that tradition was authority, that reason was authority, and that the pope was authority. And late medieval religion believed there was no tension among those authorities. They were all equally authoritative. But as Luther set to work, he began to find that there were tensions among these authorities. He found that he could not reconcile one authority with another.

His confidence first began to waiver in reason as an authority. Luther later in his life would make one of his famous hyperbolic statements when he said that reason was a whore. What he meant was not that one should never reason or that reason was not useful in conducting the affairs of this life. Rather, what he meant was that when one reflects on spiritual things, when one thinks about theology, reason will only lead you astray. Reason gets you nowhere. One has to find truth through revelation was Luther's ultimate conclusion. And so, already in the early years of the second decade of the sixteenth century, Luther began to move away from the great confidence in Aristotle and his reasoning that the medieval theologians had taught.

In 1517, about a month before his posting of the famous 95 Theses, Luther wrote some theses in September 1517 entitled *Disputations Against Scholastic Theology*. In this disputation he shows that he had reached the point *of rejecting Aristotle as* an authority in religion. One of the theses said, "The whole Aristotle is to theology as darkness is to light."[2] So Aristotle has nothing to teach us in theology.

What was his antidote to Aristotle? In these theses the antidote was Augustine. Here he was pitting, in effect, two traditions of the church against each other. What he contrasted then was Aristotle with Augustine.

At the beginning of these theses he wrote, "To say that Augustine exaggerates in speaking against heretics is to say that Augustine tells lies almost everywhere."[3] That was a revolutionary thing for Luther to say because the standard medieval way of dealing with Augustine on predestination was to say that he had exaggerated in his opposition to Pelagius. Pelagius was so bad in his theology that Augustine had to overstate his position on grace and predestination as an antidote to Pelagius. But here Luther has clearly reached the conclusion that Augustine was not exaggerating when he wrote about grace and predestination. So Luther was changing by 1517 in the matter of authority. He was rejecting reason and counterposing to that the authority particularly of Augustine as the great doctor of the church.

His thought continued to develop, and again we have the feeling that we can almost see his thought crystallize in the great debate that he entered into at Leipzig in 1519. There he confronted one of the great theologians of the Roman Church, Johannes Eck. The debate turned into a disputation especially about authority. Eck kept pressing the point that Luther could not be right when he stood against the popes, the doctors, the bishops, the councils, and the tradition of the church. What right did he have to claim that he was right and everybody else was wrong? Eck painted Luther into a corner. Eck knew the history of the church and the decisions of the doctors, the theologians, and the councils of the church much better than Luther did. Luther, in that situation where he could not answer history with history, kept falling back on the Scriptures. That after all was what Luther had been studying through the years. He was a professor of the Bible at Wittenberg. So Luther kept returning to the Bible and arguing against the history of the church from the Bible. Eck finally charged him with behaving just like John Huss. Huss was a condemned heretic. To be identified with Huss was to be utterly identified with heresy. Luther—really on the spot—seemed finally to have realized that the only absolute authority in theology is the Scripture. Tradition was not a genuine authority. Tradition was not a reliable guide to truth. Tradition did not speak with one voice: what tradition, whose tradition, which tradition? Luther came to realize clearly that Scripture alone must be our authority.

The Matter of Salvation

Similarly, over time, Martin Luther came to a fresh understanding of the matter of salvation. He entered the monastery a convinced medieval Catholic, and for the medieval Catholic, the gospel was the new law. Christ was the new lawgiver. You can see that displayed in various forms of iconography in the Middle Ages: Christ appears in various pictures looking almost like Moses with the book of the Law in his hand. The gospel was seen as a more demanding law than the Old Testament law. Luther took that all with great seriousness and saw the Christian life as this arduous road toward obedience.

Some of you may have heard of the reply of John Calvin to Cardinal Sadoleto in his defense of the Reformation. But most of us do not read Sadoleto's original letter to the Genevans urging them to come back to the Roman Catholic faith. In that letter Sadoleto brilliantly summarizes this medieval Roman position on salvation.

And since the way of Christ is arduous, and the method of leading a life conformable to His laws and precepts very difficult (because we are enjoined to withdraw our minds from the contamination of earthly pleasures and to fix them upon this one object—to despise the present good which we have in our hands, and aspire to the future, which we see not), still of such value to each one of us is the salvation of himself and of his soul, that we must bring our minds to decline nothing, however harsh, and endure everything, however laborious, that, setting before ourselves the one hope of our salvation, we may at length, through many toils and anxieties . . . attain to that stable and ever-during salvation.[4]

You see, there is the medieval picture. It is toil and worry and work to the end, in the hope that maybe one might be saved. In reaction to that pattern of teaching, to that understanding of salvation, Luther came gradually to understand the gospel.

In his famous 1545 preface to his Latin works, he reflected on his life as a monk and on how much he was trapped in this works-righteousness. He said:

Though I lived as a monk without reproach, I felt that I was a sinner before God with an extremely disturbed conscience. I could not believe that he was placated by my satisfaction. I did not love, yes, I hated the righteous God who punishes sinners, and secretly, if not blasphemously, certainly murmuring greatly, I was angry with God, and said, "As if, indeed, it is not enough, that miserable sinners, eternally lost through original sin, are crushed by every kind of calamity by the law of the decalogue, without having God add pain to pain by the gospel and also by the gospel threatening us with his righteousness and wrath!" Thus I raged with a fierce and troubled conscience.[5]

He wondered how one could not hate a God who comes only with righteous demands that cannot be met. That was the anguish of the soul of Martin Luther as a monk. It was that anguish that drove him into the Scriptures and led ultimately to what we know as his evangelical breakthrough. He came to a realization that when God speaks of righteousness, he is not speaking of the righteousness that he demands, but when he speaks of righteousness in the gospel, he is speaking of the righteousness that he gives in Christ. And Luther said that this apparently small difference turned his world upside down. Again he wrote about his discovery: "Here I felt that I was altogether born again and had entered paradise itself through open gates."[6] He said he ran his mind through the Scriptures with his new insight and saw passage after passage revealed in a new light. Luther had committed the New Testament to memory and vast sections of the Old Testament. As he went through that memory of Scripture, he saw the doctrine of justification by faith coming through.

What Luther had experienced intensely in his life was the contrast between works and glory on the one hand and faith and grace on the other. He came to talk about the Roman Church's theology of glory: the glory of the use of the human mind and reason to understand human theology, the glory of the human experience in gaining merit before God to attain salvation. This theology of glory he contrasted with the theology of the cross where a man comes to recognize that his own mind could not bring him to the truth and his own works could not bring him to God. Only on the cross, that ultimate place of foolishness, was God to be found. Luther, again in his hyperbolic manner, would talk about finding God where he ought not to be. Where ought God to be? He ought to be found in the beauty of nature, in the glories of this world. But God was not to be found there. Rather, he was to be found on the cross. But God should not be found on the cross, the place of condemnation, the place of failure. God did not belong there, but nevertheless that was where he was to be found. That was where the only hope for salvation was to be found.

So Luther's theology was very much a personal theology. It was a theology that resulted from his experience as a conservative following the advice of the church, becoming a monk, becoming a student of Scripture. From that study of Scripture and from the examination of his heart and soul, Luther realized that salvation was to be found only by grace through faith.

LUTHER'S WRITINGS

Now that experience led Luther into a public path that made of him a reformer of the church. He had to explain and to defend what he had learned and taught.

One of the most productive years that Luther ever had in terms of writing was 1520. He wrote his *Appeal to the German Nobility,* in which he appealed to the princes to take the leadership in the reform of the church since it was obvious that the bishops would not. He also wrote his treatise on *The Babylonian Captivity of the Church,* in which he criticized the seven sacraments of the Roman Church and came to the conclusion ultimately that there are only two sacraments that our Lord had instituted. Then he wrote what many regard as his best treatise, *The Freedom of a Christian.*

13

Luther did not regard that as his best treatise. Luther regarded his best treatise to be *The Bondage of the Will,* the one that we Reformed folk particularly love to read and quote to some of our Lutheran friends. One Lutheran claimed that Luther did present such a position once but never repeated it. That claim is not accurate, because late in his life, Luther said that if all his works were destroyed he hoped only two would survive, *The Small Catechism* and *The Bondage of the Will.* But many observers do believe that among his finest works is his treatise on *The Freedom of a Christian.*[7]

The Freedom of a Christian is the closest thing we have to a treatise on justification by Luther. It is a splendid work and one that reveals in more detail the hyperbolic nature of Luther's theology. We can see here Luther's love of the contrast, Luther's use of the *dennoch.*

On Right Doctrine

Luther began that treatise with an open letter to Pope Leo X, expressing the hope that Leo might still be moved to reform the church. Luther was rapidly coming to the conclusion that the pope was anti-Christ, but in this letter to the pope he did not espouse that point of view. Rather, he suggested that the pope had been corrupted by evil advisers. He appealed to the pope to see the truth and rise up to reform the church. (This approach reflected a medieval self-justification that was regularly used to excuse insurrection against one's sovereign. One claimed that the sovereign was not at fault but that the sovereign was surrounded by evil advisers.)

Luther expressed his reforming concern in an interesting way in his open letter to the pope. He said that the pope needed to be aware that his concern was not about bad morals but about ungodly doctrines. Reform in the

Middle Ages had always been directed against bad morals. The aim of reform had been to promote holy living. Luther made clear that it was a fundamental misunderstanding of his reformation to view it as the pursuit of holiness. We will see later that Luther was not opposed to the pursuit of holiness. He was in favor of the pursuit of holiness. But he was adamant that he was not seeking in the first place to challenge the morals of the church. He was challenging the doctrines of the church. The teaching of the church had gone astray. He believed that unless doctrine was rectified, the morals of the church would never be straight. In fact, Luther at one point said that the morals of the Protestants were no better than Roman morals. It was their doctrine that was better. That too I hope was hyperbolic, although sometimes looking at the present state of Protestantism, one is not so sure. But nonetheless, Luther's passion was to set doctrine right.

(Let me say as an aside that it is particularly troubling today to see so many evangelicals in America saying that doctrine is not important but that the Christian life is really important. I find that especially ironic as someone from Westminster Seminary, because the liberalism that Dr. Machen faced in the 1920s was a liberalism that precisely said doctrine was not important but that Christian living was important.)

On Law and Gospel

Luther said near the beginning of this treatise on *The Freedom of a Christian* that it contained "the whole of Christian life in a brief form"[8] and then proceeded to say that all of what he was teaching could be reduced to two propositions: "A Christian is a perfectly free lord of all, subject to none." "A Christian is a perfectly dutiful servant of all, subject to all."[9] We are perfectly free and neverthe-

15

less perfectly subject. That dichotomy is the essence of the Christian life.

First the Christian is a free lord of all, subject to none. Luther explicated that statement in relation to justification. As we live before God, as we live *coram Deo,* we are perfectly free. We are free from the law: free from the demands of the law, free from the threatenings of the law, free from the condemnation of the law. Luther was not saying that we do not need the law. We do need the law precisely to drive us from the law. We need the law to drive us to Christ. We do need the law to make clear to us how weak and hopeless we are before the demands of the law. We must be crushed by the law before we can ever understand the gospel. Luther at one point in his 1535 commentary on Galatians said that there were two uses of the law, one to teach civil righteousness and one to condemn us and to drive us to Christ. And he said that second use of the law is the principal use of the law. The second use of the law is

> the theological or spiritual one, which serves to increase transgressions. This is the primary purpose of the Law of Moses, that through it sin might grow and be multiplied, especially in the conscience. Paul discusses this magnificently in Rom. 7. Therefore the true function and the chief and proper use of the Law is to reveal to man his sin, blindness, misery, wickedness, ignorance, hate and contempt of God, death, hell, judgment, and the well deserved wrath of God.

> That is what the law teaches. Hence this use of the law is extremely beneficial and very necessary. For if someone is not a murderer, adulterer, or thief, and abstains from external sins as the Pharisee did (Luke 18:11), he would swear, being possessed by the devil, that he is a

1 6

righteous man; therefore he develops the presumption of righteousness and relies on his good works. God cannot soften and humble this man or make him acknowledge his misery and damnation any other way than by the Law. Therefore the proper and absolute use of the Law is to terrify with lightning (as on Mt. Sinai), thunder, and the blare of the trumpet, with a thunderbolt to burn and crush that brute which is called the presumption of righteousness.[10]

So the law has this absolutely necessary function for Luther.

We must realize that this condemnation function of the law is not primarily conceived by Luther as chronologically prior to the gospel. Luther does not mean that you preach the law until someone is crushed, and then you leave the law behind and move on to the gospel. Rather, Luther would say all our preaching to Christians throughout their lives must be a preaching of the law and the gospel. Christians never reach the place where they do not need the law to remind them of their sin, to remind them of their tendency to works righteousness, to remind them of the danger of living in their accomplishment and yet again and afresh to drive them to Christ. That was Luther's great concern about the law. So he could say, "For although the Law is the best of all things in the world, it still cannot bring peace to a terrified conscience but makes it even sadder and drives it to despair. For by the Law, sin becomes exceedingly sinful."[11] That was the great function and purpose of the Law. Therefore, for Luther, it was crucial to distinguish between the way the Law functioned for justification and the way in which the Law might function for other purposes. He said:

17

LUTHER AND THE REFORMATION

From this you should learn, therefore, to speak most contemptuously about the Law in the matter of justification, following the example of the apostle, who calls the Law "the elements of the world," "traditions that kill," "the power of sin" and the like. But, then he says: "Apart from the matter of justification, on the other hand, we like Paul, should think reverently of the Law. We should endow it with the highest praises and call it holy, righteous, good, spiritual, divine, etc."[12]

Luther insisted that the crucial work of the theologian is to distinguish the law from the gospel. If we do not understand that distinction, we have not understood the basics of theology, Luther said. So what was the law for Luther? The law for Luther was the demands of God. Wherever you have demand, you have law, and that law is good, that law is holy, that law is spiritual. But its effect in the arena of justification will be only to drive one to despair. There is no healing in the law. There is no hope in the law because the law only holds up the demands of God that we cannot meet, that we cannot fulfill.

On the other hand, the gospel contained no demand. Then what was the gospel for Luther? The gospel was purely good news. There was no threat in the gospel. There was only promise.

This is where Reformed people sometimes worry about an antinomian aspect to Luther's thought. We worry because we tend to read Luther as if he were speaking chronologically about the law and the gospel. We worry that he is suggesting that one should preach the law until the listener is crushed and that then one preaches only the gospel, which is only promise without any demands. Then we wonder if Luther is not being antinomian. But we must remember that Luther insisted that the faithful preacher always preached the law and the gospel. There was always demand in Luther's preaching, but it was the law that demanded. Such preaching also presented the gospel, which came as promise to encourage, to support, and to cheer; "the Gospel is a light that illumines hearts and makes them alive. It discloses what grace and the mercy of God are; what the forgiveness of sins, blessing, righteousness, life, and eternal salvation are, and how to obtain these."[13]

We Reformed sometimes have trouble communicating with Lutherans because we tend to define the gospel somewhat more broadly than they do. We do not see any great problem in including in the gospel some direction, some positive guidance from the law. But that is why Lutherans tend to think we have become moralists. They think we have put some elements of the law in the gospel. I think very largely this is a difference of terminology rather than a difference of substance between Lutherans and Reformed.

So Luther's great passion was that the gospel be understood as the gracious and good promise of God. He insisted no one compromise that truth, that no one lead consciences back to the notion that they are going to justify themselves or earn God's favor in any sense or at any point for their salvation. Luther saw this moralism as a recurring problem and temptation: "My temptation is this, that I don't think I have a gracious God. This is because I am still caught up in the law. It is the greatest grief, and, as Paul says, it produces death. God hates it, and he comforts us by saying 'I am your God.' "[14] The gospel, for Luther, declared, "I am your God for Christ's sake." The gospel was not "I will be your God if you do certain things" but "I am your God for Christ's sake." For this reason he could say, "This is our theology by which we teach a precise distinction between these two kinds of righteousness, the active

19

[righteousness of my doing] and the passive [righteousness of Christ's doing], so that morality and faith, works and grace, secular society and religion may not be confused."[15] (Luther's two-kingdom theology develops how one lives before God and how one serves in the world.)

On Faith

As a corollary to this distinction between law and gospel, Luther discussed faith. Faith was what responded to the gospel. Luther was not denying that there must be a response to the gospel. He was saying that response must never be seen as a work or a human accomplishment or a human merit. Faith, then, is that response to the gospel through which we are reconciled to God. He wrote in his treatise on *The Freedom of a Christian*, "he who has had even a faint taste of it [faith] can never write, speak, meditate, or hear enough concerning it. It is a living 'spring of water welling up to eternal life. . . .' "[16] Luther's great passion was to talk about faith, the wonders of faith. He wrote:

It is indeed impossible for me to grasp and attain to this one and *only* Redeemer from sin, Jesus, except through faith. He is and remains beyond the grasp of works. Since faith *alone*, before any works follow it, can lay hold of this Redeemer, so it must be truth that *only* faith before and without works grasps hold of his redemption, which means nothing else but becoming righteous. For to have been redeemed from sin or to have sin forgiven must be the same as being or becoming righteous.[17]

Good works, however, follow such faith (or redemption or forgiveness of sin or righteousness) as the fruit of faith. We will come back to develop that point a little later, but

Martin Luther

21

it is important to hear Luther here. While he insisted that faith alone and only faith justified, Luther made clear in his writing that good works follow from and grow from faith:

> For faith is a vigorous and powerful thing; it is not idle speculation, nor does it float on the heart like a goose on water. But just as water that has been heated, even though it remains water, is no longer cold but is hot and an altogether different water, so faith, the work of the Holy Spirit, fashions a different mind and different attitudes and makes us an altogether new human being.[18]

In another place he wrote, "Therefore faith is an active, difficult, and powerful thing."[19] This faith was no bare mental assent. That was how the medieval Catholics understood faith. But Luther's faith was life-changing, life-controlling because it put one in touch with Christ.

Luther wanted to make this point about the law and the gospel and about faith so that we would clearly understand humans to be free lords of all, subject to none. As we stand before God we are not subject to the law. We are not subject to any earthly power. We are freed before God by the gospel of his promise. Nevertheless, we are also the dutiful servants of all, subject to all. That is also the reality in which we live as we live before the world, before people, *coram hominibus.*

Luther discussed human service by saying that the law is valuable but in a deep sense unnecessary. What did he mean? He meant that when faith is real, there will bubble up out of the Christian heart a spontaneous response to God. We will love to do what God does. We will desire what God desires. We will be drawn not by threats but by love to live the Christian life. In that sense, then, the law is unnecessary for the Christian. The law is unnecessary because the law demands, the law threatens, but Christians do not need demands. Christians do not need threats. They live for God by faith.

Now we Reformed are inclined to ask whether Luther was not being a little naïve. Are Christians really that good? Have Christians really come that far? Is faith really that powerful? We must recognize that Luther was not naïve. Naïveté is one of the few charges that cannot be brought against Martin Luther. We must see that Luther based his thought on this matter on a very careful distinction that he made between the inner person and the outer person. The inner man lives by faith; he has been renewed; he has been changed so that he has a principle of living faith that does spontaneously respond to God and follow after God. But the inner man is not the whole story for the Christian. The Christian is also the outer man. He is still also burdened with an old nature. In the face of that old nature, Luther said we do still need the law to nudge us, to direct us, to force us on. He taught that we must show the fruit of the Spirit. We must make progress in Christian living, and if we are Christians, we will make progress in Christian living. This progress is primarily because of the spontaneous quality of faith but is also because of direction from the law. Luther could sometimes be difficult to understand because he moved back and forth between the inner and outer man. He contrasted them in different ways. Yet when we stand back and look at the whole picture, we can say Luther was quite right.

We as Reformed may still want to draw the inner man and outer man a little closer together and talk more positively of the law for the inner man than Luther is willing to do. Yet, I think we can have a profound sympathy for what Luther was saying. He was not fundamentally wrong. He was right to say that faith makes a difference. We do have a new nature. We do have a new sympathy for God. There is a filial response to God so that we desire to please him. We can agree that there is an old nature, a sinful nature that needs prodding, that tends to move in the wrong direction. Luther wanted to stress that the real Christian life is moving toward holiness. Luther never compromised that point. In his discussion of faith, he spoke repeatedly of the way in which faith must live itself out. He said:

> Therefore we conclude with Paul that we are justified solely by faith in Christ without the Law and works. But after a man is justified by faith, now possesses Christ by faith, and knows that Christ is his righteousness and life, he will certainly not be idle but, like a sound tree will bear good fruit. Therefore, we, too, say that faith without works is worthless and useless . . . faith without works—that is a fantastic idea and mere vanity and dreams of the heart—is a false faith and does not justify.[20]

You see there is no hint of antinomianism there. If faith has no fruit in this life, it is not a real faith and therefore it does not justify. "We say that justification is effective without works, not that faith is without works. For that faith which lacks fruit is not efficacious but a feigned faith."[21] This conviction reverberated through his writings.

On the Law as a Spiritual Guide

When we come to what we call the third use of the law, that is the law as a spiritual guide to the believer, we find

that even there Luther said things that would soften even
the hardest Reformed heart. He wrote, for example:

> We need the Decalogue not only to apprise us of our
> lawful obligations, but we also need it to discern how
> far the Holy Spirit has advanced in His work of sanc-
> tification and by how much we still fall short of the
> goal, lest we become secure and imagine that we have
> now done all that is required. Thus we must con-
> stantly grow in sanctification and always become new
> creatures in Christ.[22]

That is a beautiful statement. That is not a statement to
which we could take exception.

Some wonder whether Luther was concerned about holiness since he once said, "Sin boldly!" The statement was
frequently quoted against him by Roman Catholic apolo-
gists in the sixteenth century. They thought this statement
proved that Luther cared nothing for holiness and was indifferent to sin. They feared that he was encouraging sin.
Like all other of Luther's statements, this one has to be
understood in context. The context was this: Philip
Melanchthon one day was trying to decide what to do.
Philip was a bit of a hand-wringer, never quite sure, cautious, somewhat like Hamlet. Melanchthon went to Luther
and he said that he was afraid that whatever action he took
in a particular situation would involve him in sin. To that
agony of conscience, which led to utter inaction, Luther
said to Melanchthon, "Sin boldly." That was another way
of saying, "Do something." Luther counseled that it was
better to do something in the service of God, even at the
risk of doing something wrong, than to do nothing. In that
context Luther was not indifferent to holiness. Rather, he
expressed his passion that one must live, one must take

25

risks, one must act for the Lord. One must not be immobilized by a neurotic fear of sin.

Luther's concerns were well summarized in The Formula of Concord, the last of the great Lutheran confessional statements. In 1577, after years of theological wran-
gling, Lutherans prepared a doctrinal statement to make
peace. One of the issues addressed in the Formula was the
third use of the law. Very much in the spirit of Luther, the
Formula declared:

> We believe, teach, and confess that although people
> who genuinely believe and whom God has truly con-
> verted are freed through Christ from the curse and
> the coercion of the law, they are not on that account
> without the law; on the contrary, they have been re-
> deemed by the Son of God precisely that they should
> exercise themselves day and night in the law (Ps.
> 119:1). In the same way our first parents even before
> the Fall did not live without the law, for the law of
> God was written into their hearts when they were cre-
> ated in the image of God. We believe, teach, and con-
> fess that the preaching of the law is to be diligently
> applied not only to unbelievers and the impenitent
> but also to people who are genuinely believing, truly
> converted, regenerated, and justified by faith. For al-
> though they are indeed reborn and have been re-
> newed in the spirit of their mind, such regeneration
> and renewal is incomplete in this world. In fact, it has
> only begun, and in the spirit of their mind the believ-
> ers are in a constant war against their flesh (that is,
> their corrupt nature in kind), which clings to them un-
> til death. On account of this Old Adam, who inheres
> in people's intellect, will, and all their powers, it is
> necessary for the law of God constantly to light their

way lest in their merely human devotion they undertake self-decreed and self-chosen acts of serving God.
This is further necessary lest the Old Adam go his
self-willed way. He must be coerced against his own
will, not only by the admonitions and threats of the
law, but also by its punishments and plagues, to follow the Spirit and surrender himself captive. . . .
Therefore both for penitent and impenitent, for regenerated and unregenerated people the law is and
remains one and the same law, namely, the un-
changeable will of God. The difference, as far as obedience is concerned, rests exclusively with man, for
the unregenerated man—just like the regenerated according to the flesh—does what is demanded of him
by the law under coercion and unwillingly. But the
believer without any coercion and with a willing
spirit, in so far as he is reborn, does what no threat of
the law could ever have wrung from him.[23]

Again this statement may not be exactly the way Reformed theologians would put it, but there is a real com-
monality of concern among Lutheran and Reformed that
the law be a living reality among believers, that it direct
believers in life and help them in their obedience.
Luther's Large Catechism says of the Ten Commandments:

Here, then, we have the Ten Commandments, a summary of divine teaching on what we are to do to make
our whole life pleasing to God. They are the true
fountain from which all good works must spring, the
true channel through which all good works must
flow. Apart from these Ten Commandments no deed,
no conduct can be good or pleasing to God, no mat-

ter how great or precious it may be in the eyes of the world.[24]

There is Luther's concern for holiness.

Now we see that this principle of nevertheless (*dennoch*) in Luther came out of his conviction that the Christian life is an ongoing struggle. The Christian never arrives in the sense of totally conquering sin. Christians never arrive in the sense of utterly eliminating temptation from life, even the temptation to doubt that God in Christ is their Savior. Luther said the Christian life is an ongoing struggle and in that struggle we always need the law and the gospel. Luther taught that the Christian is *simul justus et peccator* (at the same time righteous and a sinner). The Christian is at the same time perfectly righteous before God because of what Christ has done and yet still a sinner. Luther concluded that we live with this struggle correctly when in the face of every doubt, in the face of every temptation, we turn again and again and again to Christ and the gospel. He said, "When the conscience assails you, He [Christ] says: 'Believe.' "[25] This conviction led Luther to exalt the promises of God because he had known the agony of wondering if God could ever accept someone such as he.

Today we often misunderstand Luther because so often in our day few if any seem to have that agony. The idea seems often to be, "Well, of course, God would forgive me my sins." One professor once summed it up this way: "The gospel of the average man is this: I like sinning and God likes forgiving, so the world is very well set up." Today often we do not have the agony of conscience, and therefore we do not always understand Luther's passion about the promise. It is the doubting heart that needs to cling with white knuckles to the promises of God. That is what Luther understood. He said, "I myself have now been preaching and cultivating justification by faith alone for almost twenty years and I still feel the old clinging dirt of wanting to deal so with God that I may contribute something and He will have to give me his grace in exchange for my holiness."[26] Luther saw that the central temptation is to think we can bargain with God and think we can exchange something that we have done for his grace. That idea must be stamped out by the law so that we will understand Christ.

Nevertheless, he felt in the balance of preaching, one must be careful to preach more of the gospel than of the law. He wrote:

> If you preach faith, people become lax, want to do no good, serve and help no one. But if you do not preach faith, hearts become frightened and dejected and establish one idolatrous practice after another. Do as you please; nothing seems to help. Yet faith in Christ should and must be preached no matter what happens. I would much rather hear people say of me that I preach too sweetly and that my sermon hinders people in doing works (although it does *not* do so) than not preach faith in Christ at all; for then there would be no help for timid, frightened consciences. I see and experience this: Here is a man who is lax and lazy, who falsely boasts of faith and says he relies on the grace and mercy of God and that these will no doubt help him even though he clings to sins. But as soon as death comes to him, it appears that he has never really grasped and believed the grace and mercy of God. Therefore one will have enough to do to cheer and comfort him even though he has not practiced any particular idolatry. But when the message of faith has been extinguished and the heart is

completely swamped by sadness, there is neither counsel or help. Say something about grace to such a heart, and it will answer. You preach much to me about grace and mercy; but if you felt what I feel, you would speak differently. So a frightened and inconsolable heart goes on. I have heard people speak like this when I have tried to comfort them. Therefore I would like to have the message of faith in them not forgotten but generally known. It is so sweet a message, full of sheer joy, comfort, mercy and grace. I must confess that I myself have not as yet fully grasped it. We shall have to let it happen that some of our people turn the message into an occasion of security and presumption; but others, the works-righteous, slander us on this account and say that we make people lazy and thus keep them from reaching perfection. Christ, Himself, had to hear that He was a friend of publicans and sinners, that He broke the Sabbath, etc. We shall not fare any better.[27]

For Luther the solution to presumptuousness was not just to use the Law but especially to get people to understand the gospel, to understand the grace of God, to understand what Christ has done.

Luther was a pioneer and a heroic reformer. He was also a profound theologian who will help us today to understand the law and the gospel. If you want tremendous spiritual benefit and power, read Luther. He has spiritual insights that will be a great blessing to all Christians. He will help us draw near to Christ.

2

LUTHER ON
THE FAMILY

*T*he Reformation radically changed
Christian attitudes toward marriage.
For over a thousand years before the
Reformation the dominant Christian
attitude was that marriage was a second-rate choice for
those who would not be celibate. Jerome was so critical of
marriage that he said the only excuse for it was as a nurs-
ery of virgins. The monastic life of celibacy was the "apostolic life," the life of perfection that Christ counseled.

The pioneer critic in the Reformation of traditional
views of celibacy and marriage was Martin Luther. Luther
was a monk who did not marry until he was over forty.
But his study of the Bible led him to conclude that celibacy
was not the preferred state for most Christians. He saw
widespread sexual sins among priests and monks and ar-

gued that many had adopted a life of celibacy to which they were not called. Luther indeed recognized that a few were called to the single life: "But these are rare; not one in a thousand can do it: it is one of God's special miracles."[1] He observed, "It is God's word and the preaching which make celibacy—such as that of Christ and Paul—better than the estate of marriage. In itself, however, the celibate life is far inferior."[2]

The praise that Luther lavished on marriage was revolutionary in the sixteenth century. The result was that wherever the Reformation spread, monasteries were dissolved and ministers married. The married state came to be recognized as a true calling from God, which was not the case in the Middle Ages.

Luther married Catherine von Bora in 1525, and he laughed at the insult to the devil and the pope in the marriage of a former monk to a former nun. His appreciation of marriage grew through his wedded experience. He called matrimony a "divinely noble business."[3] His gloss of Proverbs 31:10 declared, "No sweeter thing than love of woman—may a man be so fortunate."[4] He wrote, "The dearest life is to live with a godly, willing, obedient wife in peace and unity."[5]

Luther was not a modern romantic about marriage. He was aware of the difficulties of an unhappy marriage. Even a good marriage in a fallen world is full of problems: "what a lot of trouble there is in marriage. Adam has made a mess of our nature. Think of all the squabbles Adam and Eve must have had in the course of their nine hundred years."[6] His views on marriage were strongly patriarchal, and he made remarks about women that today sound demeaning—although he said things just as bad about men. But he found in marriage a divinely appointed, sanctifying institution because, as Roland Bainton put it, the family is "a school for character."[7]

Martin and Katie had six children. Luther gloried in parenthood: "Now since we are all duty bound to suffer death, if need be, that we might bring a single soul to God, you can see how rich the estate of marriage is in good works. God has entrusted to its bosom souls begotten of its own body, on whom it can lavish all manner of Christian works. Most certainly father and mother are apostles, bishops, and priests to their children, for it is they who make them acquainted with the gospel."[8] He knew its joys: "Hans is cutting his teeth and beginning to make a joyous nuisance of himself. These are the joys of marriage of which the pope is not worthy."[9] He also knew its sorrows in the death of his fourteen-year-old daughter, Magdalena: "How strange it is to know that she is at peace and all is well, and yet to be so sorrowful."[10]

The richness of Luther's humor and insight about the family can be seen in this comment about men washing diapers:

Now you tell me, when a father goes ahead and washes diapers or performs some other mean task for his child, and someone ridicules him as an effeminate fool—though that father is acting in the spirit just described and in Christian faith—my dear fellow you tell me, which of the two is most keenly ridiculing the other? God, with all his angels and creatures, is smiling—not because that father is washing diapers, but because he is doing so in Christian faith. Those who sneer at him and see only the task but not the faith are ridiculing God with all his creatures, as the biggest fool on earth. Indeed, they are only ridiculing themselves; with all their cleverness they are nothing but devil's fools.[11]

Critics of the Reformation have sometimes asked if the new evaluation of celibacy and marriage was good for women. The dissolution of convents ended the one life available to medieval women in which they were not dominated by a father or a husband. Did the Reformation limit women's choice to church, children, and kitchen? Perhaps in some ways it did, although the freedom of the convent should not be exaggerated.

Luther would no doubt thunder at his critics that they have missed the point. Most men and women will marry. Marriage according to the Bible is a good and necessary institution. It is a God-given and God-glorifying school of character for men, women, and children.

3

THE FORGOTTEN
97 THESES

The year 1992 was the 475th anniversary of Luther's nailing of the 95 Theses on the church door in Wittenberg. The posting of those theses on October 31, 1517, is usually looked to as the beginning of the Protestant Reformation. Luther's attack on aspects of the sale of indulgences captured the attention of many people—common and noble—who were tired of the greed and corruption in the church of their day. Through the 95 Theses Luther became a public figure and the leader of the Reformation.

The 95 Theses, however, were not the only theses that Luther wrote in 1517. In September of that year Luther wrote 97 theses that are largely forgotten but are known to historians as the *Disputation Against Scholastic Theology.*[1]

These 97 theses are much more interesting and important from a theological point of view than the 95 Theses.

In his 97 theses Luther shows how critical he had become of central aspects of medieval theology and how he had become convinced that the church needed more of Augustine's theology and less of Aristotle's.

Luther's first thesis must have stunned many who heard it: "To say that Augustine exaggerates in speaking against heretics is to say that Augustine tell lies almost everywhere." Augustine's teaching on sin, grace, and predestination was so clear and uncompromising and Augustine's authority as a theologian was so great that the only way that medieval theologians could disagree with him was to declare that he had exaggerated some of his teachings in confronting heretics. This softening of Augustine had been widely accepted in the Middle Ages. For Luther to attack this approach was remarkable.

This attack reflected the extent to which Luther's theology had become Augustinian. As we read on in the theses, we see Luther's specific concerns to maintain the pure Augustinian heritage. His first concern was with the nature of the will in fallen people. Luther stresses that the human will is in bondage to a corrupt nature and can do only evil: "4. It is therefore true that man, being a bad tree, can only will and do evil." The desperate condition of man is summarized: "17. Man is by nature unable to want God to be God. Indeed, he himself wants to be God."

Luther stresses that only grace can rescue humanity from its fallen condition. Man can do nothing to prepare himself for grace. Only God's electing love can prepare man for grace. "29. The best and infallible preparation for grace and the sole disposition toward grace is the eternal election and predestination of God." Luther had recovered from Augustine not only the biblical picture of man's lost-

Martin Luther

ness but also the biblical truth of predestination as the source of redemption. Man cannot merit grace. All goodness comes from God: "40. We do not become righteous by doing righteous deeds, but, having been made righteous, we do righteous deeds."

Luther sees Aristotle, the ancient Greek philosopher, as the prime destructive influence that undermined Augustinian theology in the Middle Ages: "50. Briefly, the whole Aristotle is to theology as darkness is to light." Luther attacks the method of Aristotle as relying too much on reason. (Luther would later say that when it comes to theology, "Reason is a whore.") But even more he attacks the impact of Aristotle on the content of theology. From Aristotle flowed ideas about the goodness of man, the ability of his will to choose the good, about freedom and merit.

Goodness and freedom were key theological concepts in the medieval church. The Reformation began when Christians like Martin Luther came to see the goodness and freedom of man as teaching opposed to biblical religion. In North America today the emphasis frequently is on the goodness and freedom of man. The emphasis needs to be on sin and grace and predestination. Jesus Christ needs to be exalted as sin bearer, as grace giver, as the fountain and fulfiller of God's election. Only when we again understand, love, and teach these basic truths will the church be renewed and proclaim the gospel as it should.

Let us commit ourselves to becoming better Augustinians. Let us read our Bibles, our confessions, and good Christian periodicals and books that will tell us about sin, grace, and predestination. And then let's share what we have learned with others.

4

THE CELEBRATED
95 THESES

O n October 31, 1517, Martin Luther nailed his 95 Theses to the door of the castle church in Wittenberg. This event is usually hailed as the beginning of the Protestant Reformation.

The castle church and the center of Wittenberg are still much as they were in Luther's day. But there have been some changes. The tower of the church now bears the first words of Luther's most famous hymn, "A mighty fortress is our God." Luther and Philip Melanchthon are buried inside the church. And the wooden doors to which the theses were nailed have been replaced (they were destroyed by a Roman Catholic army) by bronze doors bearing the words of the 95 Theses.[1]

Luther prepared these theses as a result of concerns he had as a professor and pastor in Wittenberg. Since 1512 he had served as professor of the Bible at the relatively new University of Wittenberg, which was founded in 1502. By 1516 he was also serving as people's priest in a church in Wittenberg. These two responsibilities led him to reflect on the teachings of the Bible and the spiritual needs of the people. Over the years he had steadily moved away from Aristotle as a philosophical and theological authority and been increasingly influenced by the Bible and Augustine.

The sale of indulgences in neighboring territories provoked him to write the 95 Theses. Indulgences were an important issue for Luther because they touched on the heart of Christian faith, namely, the forgiveness of sins.

The medieval church taught that sins were ordinarily forgiven through the use of the sacrament of penance. (Sins could be forgiven immediately by God through a perfect act of contrition, but who could be sure that he or she had achieved a perfect sorrow and regret for sin?) The sacrament of penance required three acts on the part of the Christian. First, he must make an act of contrition. There must be genuine—even if not perfect—sorrow for sin. Second, he must confess his sin orally to a priest. Third, he must perform some satisfaction or work to show his sorrow and indicate some payment for sin.

The church had come to recognize that sometimes it was difficult or impossible for a Christian to fulfill his satisfaction, and the theologians had developed the idea of an indulgence. The indulgence was an exemption or dispensation by the church from the obligation of performing a satisfaction. Later the idea of the indulgence was extended to include the possibility of a plenary indulgence—an indulgence that would cover all satisfactions for all sins. In the second half of the fifteenth century the indulgence was also applied to the dead, so that the living could obtain a plenary indulgence for the dead that ensured that the dead would be immediately released from purgatory.

In the second decade of the sixteenth century the pope authorized the sale of a plenary indulgence in Germany by John Tetzel to raise money to build St. Peter's Basilica in Rome. Although the indulgence was not sold in Wittenberg, Luther knew that many of his parishioners were traveling to buy one. He knew that Tetzel was crass in his sales techniques, using the slogan: "As soon as the coin in the coffer clings, another soul from purgatory springs." Luther was aware that some people thought that they were buying the forgiveness of their sins. He felt he had to raise questions about this financial traffic in spiritual matters.

Luther acted in a conservative manner. He prepared 95 theses for debate on the matter of indulgences. He sent a copy of them to his supervising bishop and nailed a copy to the church door for his colleagues in the university to read and debate with him. It was a common practice to nail theses for debate to that church door. It was not a revolutionary act. Remember that the 95 Theses were written in Latin, and only academics could read Latin.

The central message of the 95 Theses was also conservative. Luther did not attack the basic theology of the medieval church. He did not even reject the idea of indulgences. Thesis 71 reads, "Let him be anathema and accursed who denies the apostolic character of the indulgences." He was concerned to correct the misuse of indulgences. For example, thesis 41 states, "Papal indulgences should only be preached with caution, lest people gain a wrong understanding, and think that they are preferable to other good works: those of love." Theologically the most radical part of the 95 Theses was Luther's rejection of the idea that indulgences could be applied to the dead. But even here Luther was challenging a teaching of the church that was only about forty years old.

In light of all this, how did the 95 Theses become such a focal point in the Reformation? The immediate cause is clear. Unknown to Luther, some men took the 95 Theses, translated them into German, published them, and distributed them widely. They became a popular rallying point and made Luther a famous man. They changed Luther from an unknown monk at a minor university to the popular champion of a reform movement.

But we are still left with a question. How did such a rather academic and conservative document become such a popular focus of attention? Several factors are involved. First, the 95 Theses touched the nerve of rising German resentment against Italian domination of the church. Germans increasingly had come to feel that they were being drained of money to support the Italian church. The indulgences were seen as one aspect of the flow of gold south out of Germany.

Second, the theses reflected the growing importance of the new learning of the Renaissance. The Renaissance was a movement away from medieval ideals and an effort to revive the ancient classics of western civilization as the standard for thought and action. For religion this revival meant a renewed interest in the text and content of the Bible. Scholars were learning Greek and Hebrew, and the Bible was coming alive for them through the original languages of Scripture. Luther showed his connection with this new learning in the first two theses of his work. There he implicitly rejected the Latin reading of Matthew 4:17, which had stated that Jesus said, "Do penance." He used the Greek original, which stated that Jesus said, "Repent."

Third, Luther used the new learning to support a vital but still medieval piety. Luther wanted genuine heart religion. He was especially concerned about the religious for-malism that the misuse of the indulgences had bred. He opposed any mechanical or automatic approach to reli-gion. True religion must be the religion of heartfelt devo-tion, self-denial, and love. He drew on the medieval mys-tical tradition with its emphasis on embracing suffering as the central experience of following Christ. In theses 92 and 93 he issued a solemn warning against those who pre-tended to offer peace where there was no peace and who pretended to uphold the cross where they had not entered the way of suffering. He concluded, "94. Christians should be exhorted to be zealous to follow Christ, their Head, through penalties, deaths, and hells; 95. And let them thus be more confident of entering heaven through many tribu-lations rather than through a false assurance of peace."

The 95 Theses set Germany ablaze with a new hero who united the themes of German idealism, Renaissance learn-ing, and medieval piety. From the perspective of the Ref-ormation the irony is that there is nothing distinctively Protestant about the 95 Theses—nothing about *sola Scrip-tura, sola gratis,* or *sola fide.* Most scholars believe that Luther did not come to his evangelical breakthrough, his understanding of justification by faith alone, until the year after he posted his theses.

Still the 95 Theses do mark the beginning of the Refor-mation. The Reformation was a broad movement to reform the church of Jesus Christ according to the Word of God. It did not happen overnight. It deepened its understand-ing of the Word over many years. We Reformed people be-lieve that the Reformation did not reach its maturity in Luther's theology but rather in that of John Calvin. But the 95 Theses mark the moment when Luther and the Refor-mation begin a public, popular challenge to the medieval church. They are the beginning of the end of papal domination of the western church. They are the beginning of Luther's career as notable teacher of the Bible and reformer of the church. That makes the 95 Theses well worth celebrating as we see in them the goodness of God for the reform of his church.

5

THE POWER OF
THE GOSPEL

The year 1996 marked 450 years since the death of Martin Luther. The pioneering reformer breathed his last on February 18, 1546. He was sixty-two years old.

Luther's last word was a convinced yes to the question put to him by one of his pastors and spiritual counselors, "Reverend father, do you wish to die standing up for Christ and the teaching that you have preached?" Not long afterward he quietly and without pain died in the Lord.

The steadfastness of his faith and the peacefulness of his death were carefully recorded for posterity. Many in the sixteenth century believed that the demons came for heretics at their death and that their eternal suffering was presaged by agony in dying. The Roman church also sometimes claimed the deathbed conversion of those who opposed it. None of that could be said of Luther.

Luther died in the city of Eisleben only a few blocks from the house in which he had been born. He had traveled there even though his health was weak to try to reconcile serious differences among friends. As he weakened there he felt that his life had come full circle and that it was appropriate that he should die where he was born.

Martin Luther was a remarkable worker for the Lord. He translated the entire Bible into German. He wrote poetry for hymns and composed the tunes. He advised the great and comforted the weak. He wrote great theological treatises and commented with great spiritual insight on books of the Bible. But he probably saw himself primarily as a preacher.

He preached his last sermon in Eisleben only three days before his death.[1] The text for the day was Matthew 11:25, "Jesus said, 'I praise you, Father, Lord of heaven and earth, because you have hidden these things from the wise and learned, and revealed them to little children' " (NIV). This text allowed Luther to return to one of the favorite themes of his ministry, namely, the surprising way in which God exercises his power among his people.

God, amazingly, wants his people to listen to his Word, and he blesses his people through that Word. "Therefore Christ says, 'All things have been delivered to me,' that is, to me, to me you must be obedient. If you have my Word, then stick to it, and pay no attention to anybody who teaches and commands you differently. I will rule, protect, and save you well."

Little children understand that they must listen to God's Word, Luther contended, but the wise and powerful do not: "This is the first point of this gospel—that Christ and God the Father himself are opposed to the wise and understanding. For they vex him greatly; they mangle the sacrament and the church, and set themselves up in God's place and want themselves to be masters." Further, "everything that God does they must improve, so that there is no poorer, more insignificant and despised disciple on earth than God; he must be everybody's pupil, everybody wants to be his teacher and preceptor."

For Luther these wise and self-sufficient folk must have the law as a hammer preached to them so that they may be shaken from their smugness and indifference to God and his Word. The warnings of God's judgment on those who would improve on God's way of doing things must be clear. Only then can people really hear and believe the comforting words of the gospel that Jesus "gave himself, body and life, for us."

The chief offense of the wise in their improvement on the ways of God is their neglect of preaching and the sacraments. The power of God works through those ordinary and apparently weak instruments of the shouted word (preaching) and the visible word (sacraments). Children understand this, but the wise despise it. "When Christ established and instituted the preaching office and the sacrament of his body and blood in order that Christians should use it to strengthen and fortify their faith, the pope cried, No, that's not the way it should be; it must be wisely handled!" So the pope gave the church more sacraments and images and monasteries and fastings and good works and pilgrimages to improve on the simplicity of the Word of God.

In a statement that is vintage Luther, we can see his lament for the foolishness of people in their efforts to be wise:

In times past we would have run to the ends of the world if we had known of a place where we could have heard God speak. But now that we hear this every day in sermons, indeed, now that all books are full of it, we do not see this happening. You hear at home in your house, father and mother and children sing and speak of it, the preacher speaks of it in the parish church—you ought to lift up your hands and rejoice that we have been given the honor of hearing God speaking to us through his Word.

Oh, people say, what is that? After all, there is preaching every day, often many times every day, so that we soon grow weary of it. What do we get out of it? All right, go ahead, dear brother, if you don't want God to speak to you every day at home in your house and in your parish church, then be wise and look for something else; in Trier is our Lord God's coat, in Aachen are Joseph's pants and our blessed Lady's chemise; go there and squander your money, buy indulgence and the pope's secondhand junk; these are valuable things! You have to go far for these things and spend a lot of money; leave house and home standing idle!

But aren't we stupid and crazy, yes, blinded and possessed by the devil? There sits the decoy duck in Rome with his bag of tricks, luring to himself the whole world with its money and goods, and all the while anybody can go to baptism, the sacrament, and the pulpit! How highly honored and richly blessed we are to know that God speaks with us and feeds us with his Word, gives us his baptism, the keys [absolution], etc! But these barbarous, godless people say: What, baptism, sacrament, God's Word?—Joseph's pants, that's what does it! It is the devil in the world who makes the high personages, the emperor and the kings, oblivious to such things and causes them to allow themselves to be so grossly duped and fooled and bespattered with filth by these first-class rascals and liars, the pope and his tonsured shavelings. But we should listen to God's Word, which tells us that he is our schoolmaster, and have nothing to do with Joseph's pants or the pope's juggling tricks.

Luther, literally with his dying breath, calls the church to listen to God's Word and to find the power of God where God has put it, in the preaching and sacraments. If Luther came and preached to the American evangelical church today, his message could be exactly the same one he preached in Eisleben in 1546. So many today are looking for God and his power everywhere except in the preached and visible Word. Some fly to Toronto as a pilgrimage for holy laughter. Some embrace Rome and its old improvements on the ways of God. Others seek the powerful magic of wise sociologists at the Crystal Cathedral or Willow Creek Community Church. Still others fill stadiums to be empowered by roaring crowds or send money to some wild televangelist to get some powerful trinket in return. But the Bible and the local church's ministry are often neglected or despised.

May the legacy of Luther live among us again. May the Holy Spirit fill our hearts with a great desire for the true power of God found in the faithful preaching of the Word and the faithful administration of Christ's sacraments.

6

THE FORGOTTEN
REFORMER

*M*any influential leaders of the Reformation are largely forgotten today. One of those—especially neglected by Reformed people—is Philip Melanchthon (1497–1560). Yet if we had asked Martin Luther in the 1520s who he thought would emerge as the great leader of the German Reformation, he would certainly have answered "Melanchthon." He once said on theology, "Luther has the content, but not the style. Erasmus has the style, but not the content. Karlstadt has neither the content nor the style. Melanchthon has both the content and the style."

Luther's praise for Melanchthon is not surprising. Philip was Luther's colleague and close friend at Wittenberg University. He was brilliant, one of the greatest Greek scholars of his day. In 1521 he produced the first systematic theology of the Reformation, his *Loci Communes (Commonplaces)*.[1]

In many ways the high point of Melanchthon's leadership occurred in 1530. The Emperor Charles V was back in Germany for the first time since he had heard Luther at Worms in 1521. He summoned the Protestant princes to present their faith and to defend it at the Diet of Augsburg. Luther was not permitted by the emperor to be present at the Diet, so Melanchthon was selected as the theologian to draw up a summary of the Protestant faith and to advise the princes at Augsburg. The document that Melanchthon wrote is known to history as the Augsburg Confession. This confession first states positively what Protestants believe and then specifies certain abuses in the life of the Roman Catholic Church that they reject. This confession was presented to the emperor in the name of the Protestant princes and continues to be the basic confessional standard of Lutheranism.

The emperor gave the confession to his theologian, John Eck, whom Luther had debated in Leipzig in 1519. Eck wrote a confutation of the confession, and Melanchthon responded with his apology for the confession. Melanchthon's apology was so highly regarded by Lutherans that it is included along with the Augsburg Confession in the Book of Concord—the authoritative collection of orthodox Lutheran confessions.

Despite these great accomplishments doubts began to arise in some Lutheran circles about Philip in the 1530s. There were several reasons for these doubts. First, Philip showed that he was too gentle and diffident to provide that strong leadership that the movement needed. Clyde Manschreck's modern biography underscores that point in its title, *Melanchthon, the Quiet Reformer*.[2] It was in response to Philip's tentativeness that Luther made one of his most quoted comments. Philip was so worried about which way to act in a certain situation that he was immobilized. Luther impatiently called him to action saying, "Sin boldly." Luther meant that it was better to do something for God even at the risk of sinning than to do nothing for fear of sin.

A second reason for Philip's loss of influence in some circles was his movement away from theology. Melanchthon continued to write theology, but it was not his prime interest. He returned to his Greek studies and wrote on philosophy, rhetoric, and education. His reforming work on the school curriculum earned him the title in history of *Praeceptor Germaniae,* the Teacher of Germany.

The third and perhaps most important reason for doubts about Melanchthon arose from his theology. For some he was too gentle in his theological formulations. Two great questions have been raised about Melanchthon's theology: the matter of synergism and the matter of the Lord's Supper.

The debate on synergism arose because of changes in Melanchthon's understanding of conversion. While early in his career he had said that only the Word and the Spirit are the causes of conversion, later he said that the Word, the Spirit, and the consenting will of man are the causes of conversion. He always insisted that he was not making the will of man meritorious in the process of conversion. Still his change surely moved him closer to Erasmus and away from the strong monergism of the Reformation.

Melanchthon's position on the Lord's Supper is of special interest to the Reformed. Melanchthon showed a willingness to tolerate a wider range of opinions on the Lord's Supper than did Luther's strictest followers. After Luther's death and after Calvin became one of the dominant Reformation figures, Calvin and Melanchthon had a rather extensive correspondence on many subjects, including the

Lord's Supper. Calvin believed that he and Melanchthon agreed about the Lord's Supper. He repeatedly urged Philip to state his agreements with the Reformed publicly. Calvin believed that Melanchthon's support would greatly advance ecumenical relations between the Reformed and Lutherans. Philip probably was correct in believing that the only effect of such public statements would be to reduce his influence further with strict Lutherans.

Estimates of Melanchthon vary greatly. Luther never ceased to love and praise him. Philip is buried near Luther in the castle church in Wittenberg, his marker identical in size to Luther's. But in Concordia Seminary's library in St. Louis among the many portraits of Lutheran worthies there is no portrait of Melanchthon. Perhaps Philip was too gentle. But in comparison with Luther (whom Philip called "a violent physician for a violent age") he encourages us to be careful and temperate as well as faithful.

7

MELANCHTHON AT FIVE HUNDRED

*T*he year 1997 marked the five hundredth anniversary of the birth of Philip Melanchthon. Philip was Luther's right-hand man, trusted and loved by Luther. He was fourteen years younger than Luther but was with him from the beginning in the reforming work that Luther led from the university and the pulpit of Wittenberg.

Melanchthon was so brilliant that Luther fully expected that in time he would replace Luther as the leader of the reform. And Philip's contributions to the Reformation were of immense importance. He wrote the first systematic theology of the Reformation, his *Commonplaces*, which first appeared in 1521 and went through many later editions. He also wrote the Augsburg Confession, the foundational confession of orthodox Lutheranism. He prepared the *Apology* for the Augsburg Confession, which he with others presented to the Emperor Charles V at the Diet of Augsburg in 1530.

Melanchthon was involved in many of the leading events of the early Reformation. He was with Luther in Leipzig in 1519 when Luther first began to articulate the doctrine of Scripture alone as the authority for Christian truth. He tried to lead the reform movement in Wittenberg in 1521 while Luther was in hiding in the Wartburg. He accompanied Luther to Marburg, where they discussed the Lord's Supper with Ulrich Zwingli of Zurich and Martin Bucer of Strassburg. He became a friend of Calvin at some meetings, and they carried on a correspondence with each other over many years.

The potential of Philip's early years was not fully realized later. He proved to be too timid to lead the reforming work as Luther had anticipated. For Lutherans he was suspect because he was willing to agree substantially with Calvin on the Lord's Supper and because he compromised to some extent with the edicts of the Roman Catholic emperor in 1548. For Lutherans and Calvinists he was suspect because he seemed later in his life to give a greater role in conversion to the human will than had Luther. Many were disappointed with him that he gave his later life more to educational reform than to theology.

Still Melanchthon was a brilliant and profound theologian. On this significant anniversary of his birth it is appropriate to remember something of his achievement as a great reformer. One scholar, Ernst Bizer, has summarized Melanchthon's theology as a "theology of the promise." And indeed the promises of God in Christ stand at the heart of his religion. We can see something of the

powerful insights of his theology in the quotations that
follow.

Like Luther Melanchthon knew the horrible fear of the
conscience awakened to the reality of sin and needing
good news from God:

> Those whom conscience has terrified in this manner
> would most surely be driven to despair, the usual
> condition of the condemned, if they were not lifted
> up and encouraged by the promise of the grace and
> mercy of God, commonly called the gospel. If the af-
> flicted conscience believes the promise of grace in
> Christ, it is resuscitated and quickened by faith.[1]

PROMISE AND FAITH

For Philip the heart of the gospel was in the certainty of
the promise of God and in the confidence of faith:

> In order that it may be certain, the promise was sent
> out, and God commands that we believe and assent
> to the promise and declare that it pertains to us. It is
> necessary to confess that this is the true and perpet-
> ual meaning of the Gospel. . . . Therefore when we say
> that faith lays hold of the benefits of Christ, it is nec-
> essary to understand that people lay hold of them be-
> cause of Christ, and they must assent to the divine
> promise and believe that the promises are truly given
> for us. Faith does not signify merely a knowledge of
> history, but trust in the promised mercy because of
> Christ, giving assent to the divine promise. Paul calls
> for the kind of faith which believes all the articles of
> the Creed, particularly that because Christ suffered
> and rose again remission of sins is given to us.[2]

Melanchthon stressed that true faith rested in the promises of God:

> You do not really believe therefore, unless you believe that salvation has been promised to you also. It is definitely godlessness and unfaithfulness not to believe every word of God or not to be able to believe that the forgiveness of sins has been promised to you also.[3]

This teaching about faith he called "the chief article in the Christian life."[4]

Melanchthon testified to the centrality of the Scriptures for faith, the Scriptures that always confront sinners with the law and the gospel:

> For what is the difference between these and the condemned? What, therefore, is faith? it is constantly *to assent to every word of God;* this cannot take place unless the Spirit of God renews and illuminates our hearts. Further, the Word of God is both law and gospel. To the law threats are joined. Scripture calls that by which man believes those threats "fear," and calls that by which he trusts the gospel or divine promises "faith."[5]

Faith justifies the believer because it rests in the promised imputation of Christ's righteousness:

> The way of speaking in Paul must be observed, where *faith signifies confidence in the mercy promised because of Christ.* When he mentions the righteousness of faith, he understands a righteousness which is imputed through mercy.[6]

Melanchthon's emphasis on the confidence of faith did not mean that the believer was delivered from all difficulties. Rather faith must always be active and growing:

Faith is not idle knowledge, but needs to grow through constant battle, through calling on God, in all pursuits and dangers. May this always shine in our hearts—that God is propitious to us on account of Christ, the Mediator, and that he will help. And let us call upon him in this faith and ask him to guide us in all undertakings and dangers. In this way, faith and true knowledge of God will increase in the hearts of the godly.[7]

Philip summarized his convictions on promise and faith in these powerful words:

And when we mention faith let the mind look upon Christ and think of the gratuitous mercy promised because of him. You are to say that you are accounted just not on account of any virtues or actions of yours, but on account of something outside of ourselves, namely, on account of Christ, the Mediator, who sits at the right hand of the Father, making intercession for us. This impulse of faith in our minds is not an idle cogitation, but it wrestles with the terrors of sin and death. It fights with the devil, who attacks weak minds in dreadful ways in order to drive them either to contempt of God or to despair, like Cain, Saul, Judas and innumerable others who decided that they had been rejected by God and so hated God furiously. Others become atheists or Epicureans when they despise the Word of God and divine comfort in great troubles. They do not sustain

themselves by faith, but broken in mind they yield
to the devil, as wicked people clamor when things
are against them: "Surely there are no gods, since the
world is being ruined by blind chance." But those
who hear the Gospel—who know that the works of
God are to lead into hell and to lead back out—
sustain themselves in such a struggle by faith. They
flee to their leader, Christ. They know that he is the
victor, who crushes the head of the serpent [Gen.
3:15], or, as is said elsewhere, who destroys the
works of the devil [1 John 3:8], and who has always
been with his own from the beginning. Therefore,
helped by the Son of God, they overcome the devil
and do not depart from God.

For that is what the fight is about. The devil urges
minds to fall away from God. Faith, on the contrary,
fights lest it lose God, lest it be torn away from God. It
declares that there is a God who, although he punishes, never the less adds the gratuitous promise of
mercy on account of his Son. He gave his Son as our
advocate and promised eternal salvation. God is seen
in his Word, and when the mind looks upon the
Word, its faith is strengthened. It does not fall away
from God, but acknowledging his mercy, it calls upon
him, expects liberation, and submits to the will of
God. It does not permit itself to be torn away from
him. And praise for the victory belongs to Christ, who
helps his own, as he himself says: "Without me you
can do nothing" [John 15:5].

Those who experience these things in life and in in-
vocation [worship] are able to understand the doctrine
of faith, and at the same time to make the distinction

Philip Melancthon

that though we are just, i.e. accepted because of Christ, faith meanwhile must nevertheless be increased in us which is true acknowledgement of God, and cannot be retained without a very sharp struggle.[8]

BLESSING AND PEACE

Melanchthon like Luther treasured this biblical teaching because it brought such comfort to the soul. In his words we can feel and rejoice in the blessing and peace of the true doctrine of justification:

Although this teaching is held in great contempt among untried people, yet it is a matter of experience that weak and terrified consciences find it most comforting and salutary. The conscience cannot come to rest and peace through works, but only through faith, that is, when it is assured and knows that for Christ's sake it has a gracious God, as Paul says in Rom 5:1, "Since we are justified by faith, we have peace with God."[9]

And again:

Look at the promise of God's mercy, and with confidence in him do not doubt at all that you have a father in heaven, not a judge. . . . You now have the way in which Scripture uses the word "faith"; it means to trust in the gracious mercy of God without any respect to our works, whether they be good or bad. For we all receive of the fullness of Christ. Those who so trust now really assent to every word of God, both to the threats and the promises of divine history.[10]

And again:

> I have repeated these things because it is very impor-
> tant that this exclusive word be diligently explained,
> so that the distinction between Law and Gospel will
> be clearly seen, and *so pious minds may think that a firm*
> *comfort has been set before them and may be aroused to*
> *faith and prayer in all troubles and dangers. For this faith*
> *must be exercised in daily difficulties.* . . . Therefore faith
> signifies not only knowledge of history, but trust in
> the mercy promised because of Christ, or assent to the
> promise of grace.[11]

Melanchthon's life and theology were not perfect, but
no theologian's ever are. In spite of his weaknesses and
failures we must still appreciate the insight and strength
of his work. His expression of the theology of promise remains a great heritage of the church—something to be ap-
preciated and appropriated in our time.

PART TWO

Calvin

AND THE REFORMATION

8

CALVIN THE
CHURCHMAN

ohn Calvin was a churchman. He not only proclaimed a theology of the church but also labored to build, teach, and preserve the church. More than four hundred fifty years ago—in 1541—Calvin's service to the church expressed itself in several ways that can encourage and help us today.

As the year 1541 opened Calvin was still a resident of Strassburg. He had lived there since his exile from Geneva in 1538. He had occupied his years with writing, pastoring a French refugee congregation, developing his theology, and marrying Idolette de Bure. In 1540 the leaders of the city of Geneva had urged Calvin to take up his pastoral work there again, and in September 1541 he did return to Geneva. In his work for Strassburg and his work in Geneva in 1541 we can see Calvin's concern for the unity and the purity of the church.

At the beginning of 1541 Calvin was continuing his involvement in ecumenical conferences. The Emperor Charles V had called various theologians together to try to restore the unity of the church. The leading Protestant representatives were Philip Melanchthon, Luther's right-hand man, and Martin Bucer, the leading reformer of Strassburg. Bucer asked Calvin to accompany him. (Calvin was beginning to be recognized as a leader at age thirty-one.) Calvin's letters about the final conference in Regensburg reflect something of his attitudes about the unity of the church. He was not optimistic about the outcome but was willing to try: "Although scant, there is, however, the hope of doing somewhat."[1] Later he wrote, "Though I find my prolonged stay here to be irksome, yet never shall I regret having come."[2] Years later in a letter to Thomas Cranmer, Archbishop of Canterbury, Calvin would give fuller expression to his concern for unity, "And would that it were attainable to bring together into some place, from various Churches, men eminent for their learning, and that after having carefully discussed the main points of belief one by one, they should, from their united judgments, hand down to posterity the true doctrine of Scripture. . . . So much does this concern me, that, could I be of any service, I would not grudge to cross even ten seas, if need were, on account of it. . . . Now seeing that a serious and properly adjusted agreement between men of learning upon the rule of Scripture is still a desideratum, by means of which Churches, though divided on other questions, might be made to unite, I think it right for me, at whatever cost of toil and trouble, to seek to obtain this object."[3]

Calvin's decision to return to Geneva also reflected his concern for the unity of the church. He had never wanted

John Calvin

69

to undertake pastoral work in Geneva, and after his exile, he did not want to return. But he believed that he was called by God to that work and seeing the decline of the church without him concluded that he must go back. Still he insisted that the unity of the church would be protected by drafting ecclesiastical ordinances (a church order) immediately upon his return. These ordinances described the four offices of the church (pastor, doctor, elder, and deacon) and specified matters of worship and discipline. The issue of spiritual discipline and the church's right to excommunicate was especially important to Calvin since it was over that issue that he had been exiled. He believed that a sound church order was crucial to the unity and harmony of the church. He wrote in a letter to his former colleague in the ministry at Geneva, William Farel, "Immediately after I had offered my services to the Senate, I declared that a Church could not hold together unless a settled government should be agreed on, such as is prescribed to us in the word of God, and such as was in use in the ancient Church."[4] Calvin achieved most of what he wanted in the matter of discipline but had to settle and was willing to settle for less than perfection. In 1542 he wrote of the order adopted on discipline: "We at length possess a Presbyterial Court, such as it is, and a form of discipline, such as these disjointed times permit."[5]

As Calvin labored in Geneva to build up the church, his friend Farel was seeking to do the same in Neuchatel. Calvin had great regard for Farel's integrity, wisdom, and zeal. Yet he knew that Farel could sometimes be too inflexible. In his concern for the peace and unity of the church Calvin wrote Farel to be flexible when possible: "We only desire earnestly that, in so far as your duty will admit, you will accommodate yourself more to the people. There are, as you know, two kinds of popularity: the one, when we hunt after favour from motives of ambition and the desire of pleasing; the other, when, by fairness and moderation, we gain upon their esteem, so as to make them willing to be taught by us. . . . With reference to this particular point, we perceive that you do not give satisfaction even to some good men."[6]

For all his great concern about the unity of the church, Calvin was just as passionate about the purity of the church. One could not always be flexible. He observed the proceedings at Regensburg and saw with grave misgivings the accommodating methodology of Melanchthon and Bucer as they worked for unity with the Roman Catholics. He described their approach: "Philip and Bucer have drawn up ambiguous and insincere formulas concerning transubstantiation, to try whether they could satisfy the opposite party by yielding nothing. I could not agree to this device, although they have, as they conceive, reasonable grounds for doing so, for they hope that in a short time it would so happen that they would begin to see more clearly if the matter of doctrine shall be left an open question for the present; therefore they rather wish to skip over it."[7] In other words Calvin sees the Protestant leaders trying to devise an ambiguous formula that would not deny anything basic to Protestant belief but would be so vague as to allow apparent agreement in the present with the hope that in the future the other side might be won over. Calvin saw this methodology as flawed and dangerous: "they . . . do not dread that equivocation in matters of conscience, than which nothing can possibly be more hurtful."[8] Calvin saw such deliberate efforts at ambiguity as disastrous for the cause. Rather, in another letter he praised the virtues of a bold presentation of the truth: "Deliberately, without fear of offence, I condemned that peculiar local presence; the act of adoration I declared to be altogether insufferable. Believe me, in matters of this kind, boldness is absolutely necessary for strengthening and confirming others."[9] For Calvin unity could not be purchased at the expense of cardinal truths of the faith. Of the compromise efforts with the Roman Catholics at Regensburg, he wrote, "So far as I understand, if we could be content with only a half Christ, we might easily come to understand one another."[10]

Calvin's care for the purity of the church is seen clearly in his activities on returning to Geneva. The ecclesiastical ordinances ensured not only the unity of the church but also its purity in being governed according to the Word of God. Calvin was unwilling to return to Geneva if the basic scriptural order of the church was not guaranteed in Geneva.

His zeal for the truth was reflected in the preaching and teaching that he did in 1541. In that year he wrote a helpful work on the controverted subject of the Lord's Supper, *Short Treatise on the Holy Supper*. He also translated the important 1539 revision of his *Institutes* into French so that it could be read by more people.

What can we learn from Calvin's great labors for Christian unity and truth in 1541? Some lessons are easy. The unity of the church is important and should be vigorously pursued. Christian truth is important and must be carefully studied. Truth and unity are not separate and competing ideas but are interconnected and interdependent. Unity is unity in truth as well as association. Truth proclaims the doctrine of the unity of the church.

Can Calvin help us with our concerns for the unity and purity of the church today? Calvin clearly recognized that some issues of truth were not of enough importance to divide the church. But Calvin does not give us any specific guidelines for distinguishing vital issues from peripheral ones. He does give us some clues as to his approach. First, the source of authority for truth in the church must be recognized as the Scriptures. Truth, and unity grounded in the truth, must be based on the Bible. That conviction cannot be compromised. Second, the Scripture functions as our authority as we study its particular teachings. We cannot vaguely appeal to the spirit of the Bible. We must derive biblical truth by studying and comparing the various texts of Scripture. Third, the unity and truth of the church today must be related to the ancient church. Unity and truth are not just contemporary concerns but also historic ones. We must be unified in truth with the church of the ages. Modern innovations are likely to be heretical or schismatic. Fourth, we must be honest and straightforward. Unity and truth are not served by devious ambiguity. Only when we honestly state our views can we determine whether we can be united in truth.

Calvin's work in 1541 encourages us to love Christ's church in its truth and unity. In that church we want to serve and know the whole Christ, not a half Christ. As we study the Scriptures, we still find the whole Christ best in the Reformed heritage that Calvin among others has provided for us.

9

CALVIN ON
CHURCH UNITY

ecently in reading John Calvin's *Commentary on the Book of Psalms* I came across several interesting statements by the great Reformer on the church and its unity.

Calvin loves the church and cherishes its unity. But he also sees that his day is no golden age. Only God ensures the preservation of the church: "We know that it is a temptation which pains us exceedingly, to see wickedness breaking forth and prevailing in the midst of the Church, the good and the simple unrighteously afflicted, while the wicked cruelly domineer according to their pleasure. This sad spectacle almost completely disheartens us; and, therefore, we have much need to be fortified from the example which David here sets before us: so that, in the midst of the greatest desolations which we behold in the Church, we may comfort ourselves with this assurance, that God will finally deliver her from them."[1]

Divisions in the church should not drive us to despair, for God can heal them: "God would not suffer his Church altogether to fall, having once founded it with the design of preserving it for ever; for he forsakes not the work of his own hands. This comfort ought to be improved by ourselves at the present period, when we see the Church on every side so miserably rent asunder, leading us to hope that all the elect who have been adjoined to Christ's body, will be gathered unto the unity of the faith, although now scattered like members torn from one another, and that the mutilated body of the Church, which is daily distracted, will be restored to its entireness; for God will not suffer his work to fail. . . . The Church, though it may not always be in a flourishing condition, is ever safe and secure, and . . . God will miraculously heal it, as though it were a diseased body."[2]

We must work for unity, but we cannot compromise basic truth: "There can at the same time by no doubt that the Holy Ghost is to be viewed as commending in this passage that mutual harmony which should subsist amongst all God's children, and exhorting us to make every endeavor to maintain it. So long as animosities divide us, and heart-burnings prevail amongst us, we may be brethren no doubt still by common relation to God, but cannot be judged one so long as we present the appearance of a broken and dismembered body. As we are one in God the Father, and in Christ, the union must be ratified amongst us by reciprocal harmony and fraternal love. . . . We are to set ourselves against those turbulent spirits which the devil will never fail to raise up in the Church, and be sedulous to retain intercourse with such as show a docile and tractable disposition. But we cannot extend this intercourse to those who obstinately persist in error, since the condition of receiving them as brethren would be our renouncing him who is Father of all, and from whom all spiritual relationship takes its rise. The peace which David recommends is such as begins in the true head, and this is quite enough to refute the unfounded charge of schism and division which has been brought against us by the Papists, while we have given abundant evidence of our desire that they would coalesce with us in God's truth, which is the only bond of holy union."[3]

We should not leave the church because its members are not holy enough but only when true doctrine and worship are violated: "As we too often see the Church of God defaced by much impurity, to prevent us from stumbling at what appears so offensive, a distinction is made between those who are permanent citizens of the Church, and strangers who are mingled among them only for a time. This is undoubtedly a warning highly necessary, in order that when the temple of God happens to be tainted by many impurities, we may not contract such disgust and chagrin as will make us withdraw from it. By impurities I understand the vices of a corrupt and polluted life. Provided religion continue pure as to doctrine and worship, we must not be so much stumbled at the faults and sins which men commit, as on that account to rend the unity of the Church. Yet the experience of all ages teaches us how dangerous a temptation it is when we behold the Church of God, which ought to be free from all polluting stains, and to shine in uncorrupted purity, cherishing in her bosom many ungodly hypocrites, or wicked persons. From this the Catharists, Novatians, and Donatists, took occasion in former times to separate themselves from the fellowship of the godly. The Anabaptists, at the present day, renew the same schisms, because it does not seem to them that a church in which vices are tolerated can be a true church. But Christ, in Matth. 25:32, justly claims it is his own peculiar office to separate the sheep from the goats; and thereby admonishes us, that we must bear with the evils which it is not in our power to correct, until all things become ripe, and the proper season of purging the Church arrive. At the same time, the faithful are here enjoined, each in his own sphere, to use their endeavours that the Church of God may be purified from the corruptions which still exist within her."[4]

We must work for the peace of the church among the children of God: "God commands his blessing where peace is cultivated; by which is meant, that he testifies how much he is pleased with concord amongst men, by showering down blessings upon them. The same sentiment is expressed by Paul in other words, (2 Cor. 13:11; Phil. 4:9,) 'Live in peace, and the God of peace shall be with you.' Let us then, as much as lies in us study to walk in brotherly love, that we may secure the divine blessing. Let us even stretch out our arms to those who differ from us, desiring to bid them welcome if they will but return to the unity of the faith. Do they refuse? Then let them go. We recognise no brotherhood, as I have said already, except amongst the children of God."[5]

10

A RESPONSE
TO TRENT

*J*ustification has long been known among Protestants as the article of faith by which the church stands or falls. Justification, along with the authority of Scripture and the nature of the Lord's Supper, was at the center of debates between the Reformers and the Roman Church. Vast amounts of energy and ink were devoted to clarifying and defending the Reformation doctrine of justification. All the great Protestant confessions state the doctrine.

This chapter will examine the doctrine of justification from the perspective of John Calvin's response to the decisions of the Roman Catholic Council of Trent. This perspective illumines the essential debate between Rome and the Reformers on justification.

Today such a historical reflection is especially needed. It is needed because Christians must meditate on and be renewed in the truths of the Savior's work on their behalf. They also need to be equipped to evaluate new controversies that have arisen in the evangelical community in our time.

How could a major controversy arise on a subject exhaustively studied for centuries in which there was a clear consensus among evangelical Protestants? Part of the answer is that evangelical Christians have become ignorant about church history. With what can only be called pride, many have thought that they could dig all of God's truth out of the Bible by themselves. They neglected the treasures of insights into God's Word that have accumulated from the labors of brothers and sisters over the centuries. They have insisted on reinventing the wheel in our generation—and they have not managed to make it round.

Another part of the answer to how such a controversy could arise comes from the history of evangelical Protestantism. To summarize too briefly, from the seventeenth century on, many evangelicals have seen the greatest threat to true faith coming from formalism. Especially in the state churches of Europe many people called themselves Christians and were willing to sign on the dotted line the formal confession of their church, but their lives showed no effect of the work of the Spirit. Therefore Puritans and Pietists and later revivalists of many sorts focused on the need for greater life in the churches. This concern was valid. There was great formalism in the churches, but some of the solutions increased rather than solved the problems.

Some of the solutions tainted the gospel with legalism, implying or teaching that one could be right with God, could be justified, only by acquiring a certain amount of holiness. Such legalism tended to evoke a reaction to the opposite extreme saying holiness was irrelevant to the Christian life. The pendulum swing between moralism and antinomianism continues to our day. The extremes on either end of the swing are neither theologically correct nor spiritually profitable.

The reflections of John Calvin on justification can give us the truth and stability that will build us up in the faith. The classic reflection of Calvin on Trent will illumine the issues on justification that are always before a believer.

When the Reformation began and Luther trumpeted justification by faith alone, the Roman church was not in a strong position to respond. In the course of the Middle Ages no comprehensive teaching on justification had officially been adopted by the church. Very significant differences about justification existed in the Roman Church. Many leaders of the old church recognized their weakness on this point and urged the calling of an ecumenical council that could rule on justification as well as on a variety of other issues. This council after many delays finally convened at the city of Trent in 1545. The Council of Trent established a definitive Roman Catholic position on justification. The key elements of that position can be summarized in six points:

1. The Christian is justified by grace, but human free will, although weakened by sin, can and must cooperate with grace.[1]
2. Faith is a matter of the intellect, combining knowledge and assent to truth. Such faith, known as unformed faith, cannot justify. When faith is linked to love, then it is formed faith and does justify. Faith alone does not justify, but faith and love (which produces good works) justify.[2]

81

3. Justification is not by the imputation or crediting of Christ's righteousness to the Christian but by the infusing of Christ's righteousness into the Christian so that he becomes righteous.[3]
4. Justification finally rests on the Christian acquiring and maintaining a certain level of sanctification.[4]
5. The Christian can fulfill the commands of God.[5]
6. The Christian cannot be certain that he is presently in a state of grace, or that he is elect, or that he will finally persevere.[6]

In 1547 Calvin responded to Trent on justification in a work entitled *Acts of the Council of Trent: With the Antidote.*[7] Calvin analyzes and refutes the positions of Trent chapter by chapter. With careful theological reflection and scriptural evidence, he dismantles the Roman doctrine and states his own. Look at Calvin's alternatives to the basic points of Trent:

1. Calvin begins as Trent does with the matter of grace in relation to justification. He acknowledges that man after the fall has a will but insists that that will is dead in sin. It is not free to cooperate with the grace of God. Rather, God's grace must regenerate the will. God's grace makes man willing. Grace is sovereign and irresistible. "The whole may be thus summed up—Their error consists in sharing the work between God and ourselves, so as to transfer to ourselves the obedience of a pious will in assenting to divine grace, whereas this is the proper work of God himself."[8] Calvin especially appeals to Augustine and shows that Augustine on grace stands against Trent and with the Reformers.

Calvin wants to demonstrate that Rome's claim to antiquity for its teachings is false.

2. Faith is a crucial topic for Calvin. He rejects the Roman distinction between formed and unformed faith. Calvin denies that true biblical faith is ever just a matter of the intellect or that it is not living and justifying. Faith is not just knowledge and assent for Calvin. It is also trust. Faith justifies as it trusts the promises of God and rests in the righteousness of God. "Faith brings nothing of our own to God, but receives what God spontaneously offers us. Hence it is that faith, however imperfect, nevertheless possesses a perfect righteousness, because it has respect to nothing but the gratuitous goodness of God."[9] Faith certainly produces love and good works, but the love and good works are no part of justification.

3. Calvin wants to be absolutely clear about faith so that a proper distinction between imputation and infusion can be maintained. Christ's perfect righteousness is imputed or reckoned to us as the basis of our justification. Faith looks outside itself to Christ and his work as the only hope and strength. "But when they say that a man is justified, when he is again formed for the obedience of God, they subvert the whole argument of Paul . . . (Rom. 4:14) . . . so long as we look at what we are in ourselves, we must tremble in the sight of God, so far from having a firm and unshaken confidence of eternal life."[10] Christ does infuse his grace to change and sanctify the Christian. But that infusion has no part in justification. Only a perfect righteousness can stand in the judgment and the Christian can have

such righteousness only outside himself and in the perfection of Christ. Faith is the link to Christ.

4. A key error of Rome is to confuse justification and sanctification. Calvin writes:

> Justification and Sanctification, are constantly conjoined and cohere; but from this it is erroneously inferred that they are one and the same. For example:—The light of the sun, though never unaccompanied with heat, is not to be considered heat. . . . We acknowledge, then, that as soon as any one is justified, renewal also necessarily follows: and there is no dispute as to whether or not Christ sanctifies all whom he justifies. It were to rend the gospel, and divide Christ himself to attempt to separate the righteousness which we obtain by faith [justification] from repentance [sanctification].[11]

Calvin teaches that justification and sanctification must be distinguished or one slips into the moralism or legalism of Rome. At the same time he insists that they cannot be separated or one slips into antinomianism. Justification is not sanctification, but sanctification always follows justification.

5. No one can keep any of the commands of God perfectly. All our best efforts are marred with sin. Calvin writes:

> It is too plain, however, that we are never animated and actuated by a perfect love to God in obeying his just commands. . . . In short, the seventh chapter of the Romans disposes of this controversy. There Paul, in his own person and that

of all the godly, confesses that he is far from perfection, even when his will is at its best.[12]

The sinfulness of the best Christians makes it clear
why only the perfect righteousness of Christ, received by faith alone, can justify.

6. Certainty is an important theme for Calvin. Faith
in Christ brings a certainty of sonship to the Christian. Faith brings joy and assurance that we are
right with God. The Christian can and must be certain that he is in a state of grace. Calvin writes:

> Where, then is that boldness of which Paul else-
> where speaks, (Eph. 3:12) that access with confi-
> dence to the Father through faith in Christ? Not
> contented with the term, confidence, he fur-
> nishes us with boldness, which is certainly
> something more than certainty. And what shall
> we say to his own occasional use of the term cer-
> tainty? (Rom. 8:37) This certainty he founds
> upon nothing but a mere persuasion of the free
> love of God.[13]

Calvin also insists that the Christian can be sure of his
election:

> I acknowledge, indeed, and we are all careful to
> teach, that nothing is more pernicious than to in-
> quire into the secret council of God, with the
> view of thereby obtaining a knowledge of our
> election—that this is a whirlpool in which we
> shall be swallowed up and lost. But seeing that
> our heavenly Father holds forth in Christ a mir-
> ror of our eternal adoption, no man truly holds

what has been given us by Christ save he who feels assured that Christ himself has been given him by the Father, that he may not perish.[14]

And Calvin also argues a certainty of perseverance:

For certainly, he whose expectation of eternal life is not founded on absolute certainty, must be agitated by various doubts. This is not the kind of hope which Paul describes, when he says that he is certainly persuaded that neither life, nor death, nor things present, nor things to come, will dissolve the love with which God embraces him in Christ. He would not speak thus did not the certainty of Christian hope reach beyond the last hour of life.[15]

Calvin's response to Trent is so valuable that it should be read in its entirety. This brief summary should encourage us, however, to keep the doctrine of justification clear in our minds and central to our Christian life. Spiritual balance and power flow from this doctrine when it is rightly understood and rightly related to other elements of Christian truth. In our day when the church is so weak and confused in many ways, we must not be led astray into thinking that either moralism or antinomianism will help us. Meditating on justification will draw us closer to Christ "who became to us wisdom from God, and righteousness and sanctification, and redemption" (1 Cor. 1:30 NASB).

11

A RESPONSE
TO BOLSEC

*A*n 1551—more than four hundred fifty years ago—a dramatic confrontation occurred in Geneva between John Calvin and Jerome Bolsec over the doctrine of predestination. Today that controversy is largely forgotten, but it was a significant episode that provides a remarkable window on the character and meaning of the Reformation.

The facts of the controversy are rather simple. Jerome Bolsec, who was a Carmelite monk and doctor of theology in Paris, was drawn to the Reformation and so forced to leave France. By early 1551 he had settled in the canton of Geneva working as a physician. From early on he became a critic of Calvin's doctrine of predestination in a variety of ways and settings. The confrontation reached a new

height, however, on October 16, 1551. One of the Genevan
ministers at a regular Friday gathering for a sermon and
discussion preached on predestination. Bolsec seems to
have believed that Calvin was out of town, but Calvin had
returned early and had entered the meeting late. In the discussion Bolsec rose to criticize Calvin and his doctrine of
predestination very sharply. In answer to Bolsec, Calvin
rose and gave a detailed, and according to his supporters,
brilliant defense of predestination.

The city magistrates arrested Bolsec, and he was placed
on trial by the city. To demonstrate the correctness of the
Genevan doctrine and the unity of Swiss Protestants, the
magistrates in Geneva sent a letter to get advice from
Basel, Zurich, and Bern. The responses were extremely disappointing to Calvin: the support of the doctrine of predestination was tepid at best and the counsel of the cities
was to be lenient with Bolsec.

The trial of Bolsec proceeded despite such advice, especially charging him with attacking the religious establish-
ment of Geneva and bringing scurrilous charges against
its doctrine. On December 23, 1551, he was banished per-
manently from Geneva. He eventually returned to the Roman church and in 1577 wrote a vicious biography of
Calvin that propagated many false stories about Calvin.
Bolsec died in 1584.

The letter of the city of Geneva seeking advice from
other ministers of Switzerland provides a clear summary
of the way the Calvinists in Geneva understood Bolsec's
position: "That worthless wretch rose up, and affirmed
that the false and impious opinion, that the will of God is
the cause of all things, took its rise during the present century from Laurentius Valla; but that in this he acted
wrongly, for he charged God with the blame of all evils,
and falsely imputed to him a tyrannical caprice, such as

the ancient poets fancifully ascribed to their Jove. He then took up the second head, and affirmed that men are not saved because they have been elected, but that they are elected because they believe; that no one is condemned at the mere pleasure of God; that those only are condemned who deprive themselves of the election common to all. In dealing with this question, he inveighed against us with a great deal of violent abuse."[1] The Genevan ministers saw Bolsec as charging them with introducing theological novelties and with making God a tyrant and the author of sin. They also saw him as teaching that predestination is grounded in the actions of people rather than in the will of God.

THE THEOLOGICAL ISSUE

The position of Calvin and the Genevan church on predestination was clear and well known. Calvin had written much that showed the biblical foundations as well as the importance of this doctrine for the church. When Calvin revised his *Institutes* in 1559 he alluded to this incident as well as others when he wrote in his first chapter on predestination: "A baffling question this seems to many. For they think nothing more inconsistent than that out of the common multitude of men some should be predestined to salvation, others to destruction."[2] He wrote even more strongly in the next chapter: "Some object that God would be contrary to himself if he should universally invite all men to him but admit only a few as elect. Thus, in their view, the universality of the promises removes the distinction of special grace; and some moderate men speak thus, not so much to stifle the truth as to bar thorny questions, and to bridle the curiosity of man. A laudable intention, this, but the design is not to be approved, for

evasion is never excusable. But those who insolently re-
vile election offer a quibble too disgusting, or an error too
shameful."[3]

Calvin recognized the difficulty of the doctrine for
many: "Human curiosity renders the discussion of predestination, already somewhat difficult of itself, very con-
fusing and even dangerous."[4] Yet he saw its importance
for God's glory, for our humility, and for our understanding of the character of God's grace. He wrote, "We shall
never be clearly persuaded, as we ought to be, that our salvation flows from the wellspring of God's free mercy until
we come to know his eternal election, which illumines
God's grace by this contrast: that he does not indiscrimi-
nately adopt all into the hope of salvation but gives to
some what he denies to others."[5]

Although Calvin recognized the difficulty for many of
the doctrine of predestination, that recognition did not
make him more tolerant or patient of Bolsec. Bolsec was
apparently not a particularly acute theologian. T. H. L.
Parker commented on Bolsec that he was "a poor theologian technically."[6] Calvin's impatience with Bolsec is
clear in a letter that he wrote to Heinrich Bullinger, the
leading minister of Zurich, on October 15, 1551, apparently just the day before his public confrontation with
Bolsec. In this letter Calvin did not refer to Bolsec by
name but used him as an illustration of the kinds of
problems that he faced in Geneva. With considerable ag-
itation Calvin wrote: "A certain Dominican, a minister of
the word in a neighboring village, has emerged from the
mud under evil auspices. He bawled out openly in the
assembly that he had a dispute with me and the Church
of Geneva; and this without the least provocation. Not
content with that, he brought forward a paper filled with
foul accusations, in which I was bitterly reviled for more

than twenty times. On the matter being known, he was sent home. Emboldened by impunity, any satellite of the Council of Trent insults me now with equal ferocity. This is the communion of the Church which we daily profess. I omit other matters equally dishonourable, which I endure, not without sadness; although I am not so much moved on my own account, as on that of the public; for I see clearly that such a breaking up of all orderly discipline, so foreign to Christianity, cannot stand for any length of time."[7]

This controversy is primarily theological and focused on a doctrine important to Calvin's understanding of Christian truth and life. Calvin is insistent that his God, the God of the Bible, is just and holy in all his doing, not some arbitrary Jupiter. He is also passionate about the need for sinners in humility to recognize that their salvation comes from God alone, planned from eternity and applied sovereignly to them.

The theological issue is not the only matter this confrontation illumines however. The modern reader is struck by the rhetoric of the discussion and the strong language used. This matter of rhetoric leads us also to the context religiously that concerns Calvin at this time. That religious context of persecution, especially of the Reformed in France, leads us on to Calvin's sense of the need of a Protestant united front against Roman Catholic powers. All of these factors are important if we are to understand the Bolsec affair in context and to understand it as a critical moment in the Reformation.

Today we may look back on the language and the actions in this affair as very strong. But when we remember the context we can see how critical the issues were and how difficult the circumstances.

THE CONTEXT OF THE CASE

Calvin's letters from this period not only illumine his attitudes to the Bolsec case but also show the context in which the case played itself out. Two letters in particular, both to Bullinger, bracket the period and show the depth of Calvin's concern for the severe persecution that Reformed people were suffering in France. He summarized the situation in a letter dated October 15, 1551, in these words: "For in order to gain new modes of venting his [the King of France, Henry II] rage against the people of God, he has been issuing atrocious edicts, by which the general prosperity of the kingdom is broken up. A right of appeal to the supreme courts has hitherto been, and still is, granted to persons guilty of poisoning, of forgery, and of robbery; yet this is denied to Christians: they are condemned by the ordinary judges to be dragged straight to the flames, without any liberty of appeal. It has been decreed, that the friends of those whose lives are at stake must not dare intercede for them, unless they wish to be charged with patronizing heresy. The better to fan the flames, all informers are to receive the third part of the goods of the accused. Should any judge appear too remiss, he is liable to a penalty. The King's chancellor is to guard against admitting such to public offices. . . . All are commanded, with more than usual earnestness, to adore the breaden god on bended knee. All parsons of parishes are commanded to read the Sorbonne articles every Sabbath for the benefit of the people, that a solemn abnegation of Christ may thus resound throughout the land. . . . Geneva is alluded to more than ten times in the edict, and always with a striking mark of reproach. . . . The flames are already kindled everywhere, and all highways are guarded lest any should seek an asylum here. If any opportunity occurs, we must spare no pains to alleviate the sufferings of our brethren."[8]

The situation had not improved and was perhaps worse when Calvin wrote again in March 1552: "The king lately published an edict in which he makes unusual concessions to the Germans. . . . The king, as if he had exhausted his kindness upon the Germans, ceases not severely to oppress his own. . . . The edict has forty-seven heads. If in regard to four or five of the heads some reasonable relief were obtained, the brethren will think themselves not hardly dealt with. One for instance requires, that on holidays each with his family be present at the mass, and not only that he approve that idolatry by his gesture, and defile himself by impious and faithless hypocrisy, but that articles of the Sorbonne be read aloud at the sacrifice; and thus all will subscribe to abominable blasphemies."[9]

Calvin reacted to the Bolsec challenge out of this context. He realized that the attack on the Protestant movement in France and elsewhere was intense and threatened the very survival of the cause of the gospel. He was convinced that the hour required a Protestant united front for theological and strategic reasons. Both the peace and order of the state and the well-being of the church were at stake. This conflict also raised anew the question of the perspicuity and therefore the functional authority of the Bible in the life of the church. Calvin was always intensely aware of the Roman claim that the obscurity of the Bible required an authoritative interpreter in the pope.

A UNITED FRONT

To encourage that united front and confound Bolsec's claim for support, the magistrates of Geneva sent a letter to the ministers of Switzerland, late in October 1551, telling them of Bolsec's actions and teaching: "He made an attempt, eight months ago, in a public assembly of our church, to overthrow the doctrine of God's free election, which, as received from the word of God we teach in common with you. Then, indeed, the impertinence of the man was regulated by some degree of moderation. He ceased not afterwards to make a noise in all places, with the intention of shaking the faith of the simple in this all-important doctrine. At length he openly disgorged what poison was in him."[10]

"The Senate, however, according to our request, resolved upon consulting you."[11]

"Although it is of very great importance to us and to the public tranquility, that the doctrine which we profess should meet with your approval; yet we have no reason to entreat your confidence in many words. The *Institutes* of our brother Calvin, against which he is especially directing his attacks, is not unknown among you. With what reverence and sobriety he has therein discussed the secret judgments of God, it is not for us to record: the book is its own bright witness. Nor in truth do we teach anything here but what is contained in God's holy word, and what has been held by your church ever since the light of the gospel was restored. That we are justified by faith, we all agree; but the real mercy of God can only be perceived when we learn that faith is the fruit of free adoption, and that, in point of fact, adoption flows from the eternal election of God."[12]

The reactions to Geneva's appeal for help were disappointing. Publicly Calvin tried to keep his frustration to moderate expressions, but the severity of his sense of betrayal is clear. In his letter to Bullinger (March 1552) Calvin complained about his reaction to Geneva on the Bolsec matter: "To the letters which I received when already on horseback, I only reply that I had good reason to expostulate, especially to a brother, in a brotherly way. Consider what we

John Calvin

expected from you in the troubled state of our affairs. Consider, also, how contrary to our hopes was the answer you gave us; you may see that we had some cause to grieve. You wonder, because I utter a moderate and gentle complaint, that we were assisted less liberally than we had promised ourselves. However, I make no objection to my letters remaining buried, if they contained anything offensive."[13]

Calvin wrote to Bullinger in January 1553: "You write that you were astonished why we, annoyed by a vile and impious wretch, should ask your opinion of a doctrine which he was falsely attacking. In this impression you have been greatly mistaken, for when he accused us of holding impious doctrine, we deferred to your judgment out of respect to you. I fail to see why this should annoy you. I certainly did not think you would consider any amount of labour burdensome, which should bring so very great relief to your brethren."[14]

"Nor, in truth, did I propose dictating a formula to you, to which we desire your unqualified assent. It was enough, and more than enough, to have your approval of a doctrine which we held to be found in the word of God, nor was it our object to discuss it with skill and acuteness; so far from that, the matter, when stripped of all artifice, shows that we wanted nothing more than that by refuting the man's wicked calumnies, you should bear testimony to our teaching only what was drawn from the pure fountain of God."[15]

"Your charging us with the want of moderation and humanity, was caused, we think, by your placing less confidence in our letter than you ought to have done."[16]

"But for you to plead in defense of a man who seditiously disturbed a peaceful Church, who strove to divide us by deadly discord, who, without ever having received the slightest provocation, loaded us with all sorts of abuse,

who publicly taunted us with representing God as a tyrannical governor, nay more, that we had put the Jove of the
poets in the place of God,—to defend such man, I say, were
the extreme of absurdity."[17]

"Altogether, I feel grieved beyond measure that there is
not a better understanding between us. Indeed I was as-
tounded, on finding from your letter, that the kind of
teaching which I employ is displeasing to many good men,
just as Jerome is offended by that of Zuingle. Wherein, I
beseech you, lies the similarity? For Zuingle's book, to
speak confidentially, is crammed with such knotty para-
doxes, as to be very different, indeed, in point of moderation, from what I hold."[18]

"Although you disappointed my expectations, I nevertheless gladly offer you our friendship."[19]

In his more private and personal letter to his dear friend
William Farel (January 1553) he wrote more candidly com-
plaining of the communications from Basel "so cold and
empty"[20] and Zurich who but for earlier agreements might
have become "patrons of Jerome."[21] And of Berne he
wrote, "You know how defective they are in courage and
firmness."[22] Calvin believed by contrast this his reply was
"exceedingly temperate."[23]

Calvin summarized his passion for the theological and
spiritual importance of the doctrine of predestination in
these words:

"The *Institutes* testify fully and abundantly to what I
think, even should I add nothing besides. First of all, I beg
my readers to recall the admonition made there. This matter is not a subtle and obscure speculation, as they falsely
think, which wearies the mind without profit. It is rather
a solid argument excellently fitted to the use of the godly.
For it builds up faith soundly, trains us to humility, ele-

vates us to admiration of the immense goodness of God towards us, and excites us to praise this goodness. There is no consideration more apt for the building up of faith than that we should listen to this election which the Spirit of God testifies in our hearts to stand in the eternal and inflexible goodwill of God, invulnerable to all storms of the world, all assaults of Satan and all vacillation of the flesh. For then indeed our salvation is assured to us, since we find its cause in the breast of God. For thus we lay hold of life in Christ made manifest to faith, so that, led by the same faith, we can penetrate farther to see from what source this life proceeds. Confidence of salvation is founded upon Christ and rests on the promises of the gospel. Nor is it a negligible support when, believing in Christ, we hear that this is divinely given to us, that before the beginning of the world we were both ordained to faith and also elected to the inheritance of heavenly life. Hence arises an impregnable security. . . . Hence, if to honour the goodness of God it is chiefly necessary to remember how much we are indebted to him, they are malicious injurers of God who consider the doctrine of eternal election burdensome and vexatious. For if it is buried out of sight, half the grace of God must vanish with it. Let them clamour who will—we shall always equip the doctrine of gratuitous election as we teach it with this maxim, for without it the faithful cannot adequately apprehend how great is the goodness of God by which they are effectually called to salvation. . . . God, by His eternal goodwill, which has no cause outside itself, destined those whom He pleased to salvation, rejecting the rest; those whom He dignified by gratuitous adoption He illumined by His Spirit, so that they receive the life offered in Christ, while others voluntarily disbelieve, so that they remain in darkness destitute of the light of faith."[24]

12

CALVIN THE COUNSELOR

*J*ohn Calvin was a counselor. We usually think of him as a theologian or biblical commentator or preacher. But he was also a counselor. Particularly through a vast correspondence Calvin counseled men and women, helping them to face various trials ranging from sickness to religious persecution.

In his counsel to the persecuted—largely to Reformed brothers and sisters in France—Calvin labored to build up the faith of those facing imprisonment and death. Calvin knew the temptation to renounce the faith to save one's life. He knew the ferociousness of the persecutors and the subtleties of Satan seeking to overturn faith. He wrote many letters of exhortation and encouragement. His counsel was always personal, yet it reflected a common perspective on how to build up faith in the face of difficulty.

Calvin recognized that faithfulness does not come naturally. Living for Christ is always difficult: "If I would live to Christ, this world must be to me a scene of trial and vexation: the present life is appointed as the field of conflict." The theme of conflict is often presented by Calvin in military language. The Christian is "called to combat."

In the combat of the Christian life Calvin wrote that the greatest enemy we have is the weakness of our flesh: "But the capital point is that instead of indulging this weakness we should seek to shake it off and be re-animated by the Spirit of God. I say then that nothing is more opposite to Christianity, of which we make a profession, than that when the Son of God our captain calls us to the combat, we should be not only cold and faint hearted, but seized with such consternation as to desert his standard. Let us then strive against our flesh, seeing that it is our greatest enemy, and that we may obtain pardon of God let us not pardon ourselves, but rather let us be our own judges to condemn ourselves."

The way to strengthen the weakness of our flesh is to seek our strength in God. God's strength comes to us particularly through earnest prayer and careful attention to the Word of God. Calvin wrote: "May the reliance which God commands us to have in his grace and in his strength always be to you an impregnable fortress; and for the holding fast the assurance of his help, may you be careful to walk in his fear, although, when we have made it our whole study to serve him, we must always come back to this conclusion, of asking pardon for our shortcomings. And inasmuch as you know well from experience how frail we are, be ever diligent to continue in the practice which you have established, of prayer and hearing of the holy word, to exercise you, and to sharpen and confirm you more and more."

Calvin at times became specific on how Christians have to take themselves in hand to make progress in overcoming weakness and fear. He knew that the struggle took different forms in different people, but he also knew that the basic solution was the same for all: "Many are overcome, because they allow their zeal to grow cold, and run off in self-flattery. Others, on the contrary, become so alarmed when they do not find in themselves the strength they wish, that they get confused, and give up the struggle altogether. What then is to be done? Arouse yourself to meditate, as much upon the promises of God, which ought to serve as ladders to raise us up to heaven, and make us despise this transitory and fading life, as upon the threatenings, which may well induce us to fear his judgments. When you do not feel your heart moved as it ought to be, have recourse, as to a special remedy, to diligently seeking the aid of Him without whom we can do nothing. In the meantime, strive to your utmost, blaming coldness and weakness, until you can perceive that there is some amendment. And in regard to this, great caution is required so as to hold a middle course, namely, to groan unceasingly, and even to woo yourself to sadness and dissatisfaction with your condition, and to such a sense of misery as that you may have no rest; without, at the same time, any doubting that God in due time will strengthen you according to your need, although this may not appear at once."

At the same time that Calvin stressed the reality of the struggle and the necessity of constant battle, he also repeatedly reminded Christians that they should be assured of God's care and love. The aim of the promises and exhortations of Scripture were to support and reinforce the assurance inherent in true faith. Calvin encouraged the persecuted to be assured from God's providential care of them ("an impregnable fortress") and the rich promises of God's Word. Calvin also directed the suffering to find assurance in the Holy Spirit's work in their lives: "You know, however, in what strength you have to fight—a strength on which all those who trust, shall never be daunted, must less confounded. Even so, my brothers, be confident that you shall be strengthened, according to your need, by the Spirit of our Lord Jesus."

The power of Calvin's spiritual counsel was in the fine balance that he maintained between his insistence on militant faithfulness in the real battles of the Christian life and his constant reminders of the assurance of victory that Christians have in Christ. That spiritual counsel is as good today as it was in the sixteenth century. Today Christians can face every difficulty strengthened in the same ways that Calvin counseled long ago.

13

THE FRENCH
REFORMATION

odern France is dominated religiously by skepticism or Roman Catholicism. As one scholar put it, all modern Frenchmen seem to be followers of either Descartes or Pascal. But four hundred years ago France was experiencing a powerful reformation in its religious life, and many Frenchmen were followers of John Calvin.

France produced some of the greatest religious thinkers of the sixteenth century. Lefevre d'Etaples was an important student of the Bible and led efforts to purify the moral life of the Roman Catholic Church. John Calvin and Theodore Beza were, of course, two of the greatest theologians of the Reformed church. But the ferment in France was not limited to a few brilliant leaders. The Reformation became a widespread popular movement with major consequences for the history of France. The story of the Reformed church in France is not often remembered in our time, but we should pause to celebrate the four-hundredth anniversary of one of the great moments in the French Reformation. In 1598 King Henry IV issued the Edict of Nantes, which guaranteed a variety of religious liberties for French Huguenots.

The years leading up to 1598 were eventful. The Reformed church began to grow significantly in France in the 1550s. Graduates of the Genevan Academy became missionaries in France. The students joked in Geneva that their diploma was their death certificate because so many of them died as martyrs in France. The French Reformed Church was one of the churches in those years "under the cross," that is, a church suffering persecution. Many of the martyrs, both ministers and other members of the church, died with remarkable courage. So many went to the stake singing psalms that their executioners began tearing out their tongues in prison to keep them from singing.

In spite of the fierce opposition—in some ways because of it—from the state and the Roman Catholic Church, the Huguenot movement grew and became very large in certain areas of France. It is estimated that by 1562 the Reformed church had three million members out of a total French population of twenty million.

The size and power of the Reformed church created new challenges, some from within the church and some from without. Internally the church found that increasingly influence was passing from the ministers to the nobility that had been converted. (By 1562 it is estimated that half of the French nobility had identified with the Huguenot cause.) For some of the nobility, conversion to the Reformed faith was sincere and deep. For others, however, the church provided a rationale for their opposition to the king and efforts to limit his authority. Outside the church the state and powerful Roman Catholic nobles wanted to contain or destroy the Protestants and weaken the Reformed nobility. The result of this complex situation was a time of intermittent civil war in France, beginning in 1562 and ending in 1594, known as the Wars of Religion.

The Wars of Religion brought hardship to many in France and confused the religious issues with political ones. On the Reformed side one of the nobles who stood with the greatest integrity and faith was Jeanne d'Albret. On her mother's side she was the niece of King Francis I, the great Renaissance king of France. From her father she inherited the kingdom of Navarre and was its queen. (Navarre was a small kingdom between France and Spain.) Her husband, Antoine de Bourbon, was a direct descendant of King Louis IX and so related to the French royal family, "a prince of the blood." Jeanne and her husband had a son, Henry. She and Antoine joined the Reformed church in 1560, but in time he repudiated that decision for political reasons. When Jeanne was asked if she too would return to the Roman church, a contemporary recorded that "she finally replied that, rather than ever go to Mass, if she held her kingdom and her son in her hand, she would throw them both to the bottom of the sea."

The success of the Reformed church led to a conspiracy against it planned by King Charles IX and some of his closest advisors. On St. Bartholomew's Day, August 1572, a massacre began of Protestants in Paris and spread to other parts of France. Thousands of Reformed Christians and many of the leaders of the movement were slaughtered. In some ways the church never fully recovered. Still the church survived and seemed to grow strong again.

In 1589 King Henry III of France died without a son. The next in line to the throne was Henry of Navarre, the son of

Jeanne d'Albret, himself a Protestant. To many it seemed that his succession meant that France would become a Protestant nation. But not all in France recognized Henry's claim on the throne and years of difficulty followed. By the spring of 1593 Henry had gained control of all of France except Paris. Paris was the citadel of Roman Catholic resistance. Henry could have taken the city by force, but the cost in lives and morale would have been tremendous. He decided instead to gain the support of Paris by becoming a Roman Catholic. He supposedly said, "Paris is well worth a Mass." With that statement Henry showed that he shared more of the political expediency of his father than the religious commitment of his mother.

As early as 1573 Henry had concluded that the only way out of religious conflict for France was some form of freedom of religion. Such an idea was foreign to most people in sixteenth-century Europe. Most Europeans believed that the state should support and enforce true religion. Only true religion could hold the fabric of society together. Henry's idea of religious freedom was bound to be controversial.

Still, on April 13, 1598 Henry issued the Edict of Nantes giving specific freedoms and privileges to the French Huguenots. The document is complicated and runs to almost one hundred pages. He granted complete liberty of conscience in religion to all of his subjects. He granted the right to public worship for the Reformed in various cities and towns throughout France but forbade such worship in Paris. He declared that the Reformed could hold public office, could attend university, and could print Bibles and some other religious literature. He agreed to pay the salaries of the Reformed ministers out of public funds. He also permitted Protestants to fortify and defend with Protestant troops 103 towns in France at state expense.

The intent of the edict was to put an end to conflict in France by securing the rights of the Reformed church to exist, but not making it too easy for it to grow. For a number of years it succeeded in that goal. The Reformed church, however, continued to face internal and external problems.

Internally the church saw its numbers decline to around 1.3 million by 1620. The problems of living in a predominantly Roman Catholic society also divided the church. Some believed that the church needed to be firm and uncompromising in its proclamation of the Reformed faith. Others wanted to be prudent, minimizing Reformed distinctives. From those who were prudent emerged the teachings known as Amyraldianism, which softened and weakened confessional Calvinism.

Externally the Reformed saw the Edict of Nantes amended around 1628 by Cardinal Richelieu in the name of King Louis XIII. Richelieu removed the section that allowed Protestants to hold fortified cities, arguing that the Reformed were using that privilege to create a state within the state and to foment rebellion against the king. Other Protestant privileges remained, but in the coming decades the church continued to decline.

Unexpectedly in 1685 King Louis XIV revoked the Edict of Nantes. He did that in the name of the medieval ideal of a religiously unified state. He declared that the edict was no longer needed as only Roman Catholics were to be found in the realm! As a result many French Protestants emigrated from France, moving to the American colonies, to England, or to the Netherlands. These emigrants were, according to many historians, the backbone of the French middle class, and their loss contributed to the economic polarization of France and ultimately to the French Revolution. How different history might have been had Henry

IV held to the faith of his mother, or if his heirs had upheld his Edict of Nantes.

The Edict of Nantes was one of the first political efforts in Europe to move toward freedom of religion. It attempted not to drive religion from the public arena but to create space for more than one religion. It was not ultimately successful for France or for the Reformed church there. But its recent four hundredth anniversary (in 1998) calls us to consider again the importance and difficulty of creating and maintaining religious freedom. It also calls us to remember the heroic witness of so many in the Reformed Church of France to the truth of the gospel.

14

AN INTERNATIONAL
REFORMER

ne great servant of Christ whom we ought to remember is Peter Martyr Vermigli. He was born five hundred years ago on September 9, 1499, in Florence, Italy. Peter Martyr is little remembered today, but in his day he was widely recognized for his brilliance, his learning, his piety, and his influence. By reviewing his life and work we can see again the amazing complexity and interconnectedness of the Reformation and see how God used one man to advance the cause of his truth.

Vermigli was born in Florence at a moment of great accomplishment and turmoil in the history of that city. The Renaissance was at its height, and Florence was in many ways its capital. The city produced or nurtured such great artists as Botticelli (1444–1510), Leonardo da Vinci

(1452–1519), Raphael (1483–1520), and Michelangelo (1475–1564). The Renaissance thinker Giovanni Pico della Mirandola (1463–1494), who wrote the famous *Oration on the Dignity of Man*, had studied and died in Florence. In the year of Vermigli's birth the great Florentine Platonist Marsilio Ficino died.

Politically Florence had flourished under the rule of Lorenzo di Medici, the Magnificent, from 1469–92. After his death turmoil came, as France invaded Italy and the city struggled for independence and liberty. In this time of trouble arose the remarkable monk Girolamo Savonarola. In the years between 1491 and 1498 he grew to become the most important influence in the city, preaching for religious renewal and criticizing the papacy. He was executed in 1498, the year before Vermigli's birth.

Peter Martyr grew up in this great city in these days of vitality and difficulty. In 1514 he entered an Augustinian monastery, dedicating himself to become a monk in one of the most rigorous monastic orders. The church recognized his intellectual gifts and sent him to study at the University of Padua (1518–26), where he concentrated on Aristotelian philosophy and the Fathers of the ancient church. He was ordained to the priesthood in 1525. He became known as a powerful preacher and was advanced in his order. From 1533 to 1537 he served as an abbot in Spoleto and from 1537 to 1541 as an abbot in Naples.

During this time his theology developed in the same direction as that of the Protestant Reformers in the north, although it is difficult to trace the sources of influence on him. Clearly he was influenced by Paul, Augustine, and the late medieval theologian Gregory of Rimini. He came to a strong conviction about double predestination, and he also moved to Protestant views of justification and the Lord's Supper.

PETRVS MARTYR.

Tuscia te pepulit, Germania et Anglia fouit,
Martyr quem extinctum, nunc tegit Heluetia.
Discere qua si vera volent, re et nomine dicent,
Hic fideus Christi (credite) Μαρτυρ eius.

Cum priuall.

Peter Martyr Vermigli

The decade of the 1530s was one in which many leaders of the Roman Catholic Church recognized that the church needed improvement. Pope Paul III (pope from 1534 to 1549) encouraged reflection on moral reform in the church and that allowed some room for men like Vermigli to speak in cautious ways about doctrinal reform as well.

In 1541 Vermigli became a prior in Lucca, where he found a great receptivity to reforming ideas and where he preached and taught Reformation doctrine. There he came into contact and influenced a number of important Italian theologians. Emmanuel Tremellius, a converted Jew from Ferrara, worked with him and taught Hebrew. Tremellius would later teach as a Protestant in Cambridge and Heidelberg. The great theologian Girolamo Zanchi was converted to Protestantism in Lucca, as were the Diodati and Turrettini families. From these families would come noted theologians: Giovanni Diodati represented Geneva at the Synod of Dort, and Francis Turretin was the great Genevan systematician.

In September 1541 Pope Paul III and the Emperor Charles V met in Lucca to discuss the state of Europe (Budapest had fallen in August to the advancing Turks) and the state of the church. Joining them was Cardinal Contarini, just returned to Italy from the Colloquy at Regensburg, where he had tried to negotiate a religious settlement with Philip Melanchthon and Martin Bucer (with the young John Calvin also in attendance). Contarini stayed with Vermigli while in Lucca, and it would be fascinating to know the character of their conversations.

Paul III became more defensive about calls for reform in the church. He encouraged Cardinal Carrafa, who in 1555 became Pope Paul IV, to establish a vigorous Inquisition in Italy. Vermigli increasingly sensed that the freedom he had enjoyed in Lucca was coming to an end and that his choices for the future were probably death, apostasy from his Protestant convictions, or exile. He chose exile, leaving Lucca on August 12, 1542. He took leave of friends and associates as he traveled north and arrived finally in Strassburg in November 1542. There Bucer invited him to teach in the place of Wolfgang Capito, who had died the previous year.

The decision of Peter Martyr to identify openly with the Reformed cause was remarkable. He was already forty-three, and most who courageously joined the Reformed church did so at a younger age. He had a promising career in the Roman church and left great opportunities behind. But the Lord was to open for him remarkable positions of service and influence for the Reformed faith in the last twenty years of his life.

He served in Strassburg from 1542 to 1547, sharing in the work that Martin Bucer had done there to reform the church. In 1547 he received an invitation from Archbishop of Canterbury, Thomas Cranmer, to teach as a Regis professor at Oxford. There he taught powerfully on the Reformed view of the Lord's Supper, helped Cranmer and others with the 1552 revision of the Book of Common Prayer, and aided Bishop Hooper in the discussion of the use of vestments in the church. When King Edward VI was succeeded on the throne by his half-sister Mary (known to history as bloody Mary), Vermigli again had to move to escape Roman Catholic persecution. He returned to Strassburg (1553–56) and then settled finally in Zurich, where he taught and worked with the distinguished Reformer Heinrich Bullinger. He was widely regarded as one of the greatest Reformed authorities on the Lord's Supper and so was invited to the Colloquy of Poissy in 1561. There he and Theodore Beza defended the Reformed cause before the king and queen mother of France. He also seems to have had a significant influence on Zacharius Ursinus as he was moving from a Lutheran to a Reformed theology. When Vermigli was invited to teach in Heidelberg, he recommended Ursinus in his place. Perhaps Peter Martyr deserves to be called a grandfather of the Heidelberg Catechism.

At the age of sixty-three his body began to weaken and death approached. He had lived a most remarkable life that had led him to live in many parts of Europe and to know and influence many of the most important figures of his day. His great talents and learning he dedicated to Christ in teaching, preaching, and writing (especially on the Lord's Supper and commentaries on the Pentateuch, Judges, 1 and 2 Samuel, 1 and 2 Kings, Romans, and 1 Corinthians). Excerpts from his writings circulated widely as *Loci Communes* published in Latin in 1576 and in English in 1583. Josiah Simler, who preached a funeral oration for him, aptly named him "an ambassador of Jesus Christ, to divers cities and nations."[1]

Simler recorded the final hours of Vermigli's life and his own last words: "And on the day before he died, some of us his friends being present with him, and specially Bullinger among the rest, he lay a certain space meditating with himself; then turning unto us he testified with speech plain enough that he acknowledged life and salvation in Christ alone, who was given by the Father an only favour unto mankind; and this opinion of his he declared and confirmed with reasons and words of scriptures; adding at the last, This is my faith, in this will I die; but they which teach otherwise and draw men any other way, God will destroy them." These words show the seriousness of his faith and his intense sense of the spiritual conflict of his times. His remarkable life and testimony deserve to be remembered.

PART THREE

Confessions
AND THE REFORMATION

15

A Catechism from Heidelberg

The city of Heidelberg is one of the most beautiful and charming in the world. Built in the Neckar River valley, the city looks across the river to rising hills covered with green. Today the city has a well-preserved renaissance center dominated by the Holy Ghost Church where Caspar Olevianus preached. The University of Heidelberg, where Zacharias Ursinus once taught, still is important to the city. Dominating the city visually is the great castle of the electors of the Palatinate, now partly in ruin but still a magnificent sight.

The glories of Heidelberg were not damaged during the Second World War. The Germans did not make it a military center, and an American leader who had studied in Heidelberg urged that the city be spared. As a result a visit to Heidelberg allows one to experience something of a six-teenth-century city, an experience that is quite rare in modern Europe.

In the sixteenth century Heidelberg was an important city. It was the capital of a territory called the Palatinate. (In those days Germany was called the Holy Roman Empire. The emperor had limited powers to control the hundreds of territories in the empire. Each local territory had its own ruler, laws, and customs.) The local ruler of the Palatinate was an elector. As elector—the most distinguished title a ruler could bear—he was one of seven rulers who voted in the election of a new emperor. The Palatinate was one of the most politically significant territories in the empire.

As the Reformation spread in Germany, it began to have an impact in the Palatinate as well. (Philip Melanchthon, Luther's close associate, was born in the Palatinate.) In 1545, the story goes, so many people had been attracted to the Reformation cause that the congregation in the Holy Ghost Church broke out into singing a Reformation song, "Redemption has come to us." Seeing the sympathy for the Reformation, the Elector Frederick II ordered an end to the Mass being celebrated in the city and allowed the city to move more and more into the Protestant orbit. Shortly before his death in 1556 the elector became a Protestant.

The next elector was Otto Henry (1556–59). Today he is best remembered for making some of the most beautiful architectural additions to the castle. He contributed to religious tensions in the city by appointing Tileman Hesshusius as superintendent of the churches. Hesshusius was a strict Lutheran and soon sharply alienated other Protestants (Melanchthonian Lutherans, Zwinglians, Calvinists).

After a brief reign, Otto Henry was succeeded by Frederick III, known to history as Frederick the Pious. Frederick was born in 1515 and reared a devout Roman Catholic. In his early years as elector he became a Protestant through the influence of his wife and the tragic drowning of a son. Frederick came increasingly to a Reformed theological conviction. He dismissed the troublesome Hesshusius and sought some effective Reformed leadership for his territory. In 1561 Olevianus became court preacher—he was only twenty-four years old. He had become a Protestant while studying in his teen years in France. Later he studied at Geneva and Zurich. He had known the son of the elector and had tried to save him when he drowned.

Frederick also appealed to the great Peter Martyr Vermigli, then at Zurich, to come to Heidelberg to teach. (Peter Martyr is not well remembered by the Reformed any more, but in the sixteenth century he was rightly counted a Reformed theologian equal to Calvin and Beza.) Martyr declined the invitation but recommended Ursinus in his place. Ursinus arrived in Heidelberg in 1561—he was only twenty-six years old. Ursinus had been born in Breslau in Silesia in 1534. From 1550 to 1557 he studied with Melanchthon in Wittenberg and was deeply influenced by Melanchthon. (Luther had died in 1546.) In 1557 and 1558 Ursinus traveled and met John Calvin in Geneva and Peter Martyr Vermigli in Zurich. In 1560 he spent some time studying with Martyr, who seemed to have helped Ursinus move to a more decidedly Reformed position.

Frederick gathered remarkable young talent to lead the reform of the Palatinate church. He set out to move his church in a more Reformed direction. In 1561 Frederick agreed to what the Reformed called the purification of the churches. All crucifixes, pictures, altars, baptismal fonts, and organs were removed from the churches that God might be worshiped without the distractions of human contrivances.

The elector also recognized the need of a catechism for his churches. Many different ones were being used, and he wanted greater uniformity of religious instruction for his people. He also wanted to oppose the growing influence in Germany of the strict Lutherans and their doctrine of ubiquity. (Ubiquity is the doctrine that the humanity of Jesus partakes of the divine attribute of omnipresence so that the flesh and blood of Jesus can be in the bread and wine of the Lord's Supper.)

To write his new catechism for the Palatinate Frederick appointed a committee that included Ursinus and Olevianus. The recent work of Professor Fred Klooster has shown that it seems most likely that Ursinus was the principal author of the catechism. Ursinus had a special interest in catechisms, having written two before the Heidelberg Catechism. He also later devoted much of his energy to lecturing on the catechism in his college teaching. It has also been suggested that Ursinus was a man of melancholy temperament and that the central theme of Christian comfort in the catechism reflected his spiritual struggles.

The Heidelberg Catechism followed the tradition of medieval catechisms by focusing on the Apostles' Creed, the Ten Commandments, and the Lord's Prayer. But it developed its exposition of these statements in a clear Reformed structure. Its division into sections on sin, salvation, and service reflect a Protestant understanding of grace, and its particular answers constantly draw the reader to the spiritual importance and relevance of its teaching.

Frederick was not entirely pleased with the catechism initially. He believed that a strong statement was needed to contrast the Reformed view of the Lord's Supper with the Roman Catholic view of the Mass. So in 1563 a second edition of the catechism was issued with a new question (question 80) added. The new addition read, "The Lord's

Supper testifies to us that we have a full pardon of all sin by the only sacrifice of Jesus Christ, which he himself has once accomplished on the cross. But the mass teaches that the living and the dead have not the pardon of sin through the suffering of Christ, unless Christ is also daily offered for them by the priests. So that the mass at bottom is a denial of the one sacrifice and suffering of Jesus Christ."

These words were still not strong enough for Frederick, and so a third edition of the catechism was produced in 1563 with the wording of the catechism that is now familiar. Question 80 concludes of the Mass that it is a "cursed idolatry."

This eightieth question has been subjected to a great deal of criticism in the twentieth century. Critics charge that it is out of character with the positive spirit of the rest of the catechism and is unnecessarily severe to the Roman position. Neither of these criticisms is entirely fair. We must remember that to this day the priest at a Roman Mass holds up the consecrated bread and declares, "Behold the Lamb of God which takes away the sins of the world," and the people are expected to worship the consecrated bread. Our Reformed forebears properly called this idolatry, and all idolatry is cursed.

Also the catechism is critical of other viewpoints, even if usually that criticism is implicit rather than explicit. The strict Lutheran doctrine of ubiquity is criticized in questions 47 and 48, and a Baptist view of baptism is criticized in question 74. Examples of this implicit criticism could easily be multiplied.

Those responsible for the preparation of the catechism were attacked severely in their day and at great risk defended the catechism. In 1556 some princes attacked Frederick at the imperial Diet of Augsburg insisting that the catechism taught doctrines that were illegal in the empire.

Frederick replied that he upheld the Augsburg Confession and therefore was in conformity with the laws of the empire. He also stated that he would rather die than abandon his catechism. His position was upheld by the diet.

Others also suffered for the catechism. When Frederick died in 1576 he was succeeded by his son Lewis. Lewis was a strict Lutheran and began to exile from his territory the Reformed leaders of the church. Olevianus was dismissed early, and Ursinus was the last to go in 1578. Ursinus withdrew to the city of Neustadt, under the protection of Prince Casimir. There he spent the last years of his life teaching theology and lecturing on the catechism. After his death in 1583 his student David Pareus gathered and edited his lectures for publication as Ursinus's *Commentary on the Heidelberg Catechism*.[1] This commentary remains an invaluable resource for the study of the catechism.

From the beginning in 1563 the catechism was appointed not only for the instruction of the young but also to be preached regularly in the churches. The preaching of the catechism has remained important in the churches that treasure the catechism. The profound insights and summaries of doctrine found in the catechism continue to build the faithful up in the truth, generation after generation.

Philip Schaff, the great German Reformed church historian, offered high praise for the Heidelberg Catechism when he wrote, "It combines Calvin's strength and depth without his severity, Melanchthon's cordiality and warmth without his indecision, Zwingli's simplicity and clearness without his cool sobriety and aversion to the mystics." The strengths of the catechism remain needed by the church today more than ever. In an age that is often opposed to theology, the Heidelberg Catechism is a clear, warm, attractive presentation of the great truths of the Reformation, which are the great truths of the gospel.

16

CANONS
FROM DORT

For many members of the Christian Reformed Church the Canons of Dort have remained largely ignored at the back of the *Psalter Hymnal.* Unlike the Heidelberg Catechism, the canons have little or no liturgical use in the church. Neither do they provide a concise summary of the faith as does the Belgic Confession. Rather, the canons, with their detailed and extensive exposition of several vital points of Reformed Christianity, have guided the church in its understanding of the sovereign grace of God.

In recent years the canons have attracted the attention of several detractors who suggest that the canons are not all that they could be. Even some ministers who are bound by oath to the doctrinal standards of the church suggest that the canons represent a theology that is abstract, speculative, and systematic in a scholastic rather than biblical manner. Critics fear that the canons undermine either the freedom or the justice of God.

Beyond these theological concerns are practical ones: Can the doctrines of grace expressed in the canons be preached effectively? Is evangelism in the church inevitably crippled by the kind of theology found in the canons?

These critical questions go to the root of the Reformed faith. It is time to reexamine the Canons of Dort. Under the light of Scripture, the church must determine whether this binding confessional standard should be amended or the critics recalled to the truth.

This chapter does not attempt this biblical reexamination. Indeed, the biblical evidence offered in the works of Herman Bavinck and Louis Berkhof seems abundantly adequate.

Rather, the intent here is to present the canons in a historical context that will provide a perspective and focus for discussions of their theological relevance to the life of the church today. We will first address the theological climate that gave birth to the canons, then the situation to which the canons spoke. Such a historical investigation may assist the church in determining whether the modern critics of the canons provide keener theological insight into biblical religion than did the writers of the canons. Following good Reformed tradition, this chapter presents five points on the Synod of Dort.

THE COMPOSITION OF THE SYNOD

The National Synod of the Dutch Reformed Church assembled at Dordrecht on November 13, 1618, to confront a major crisis in the churches. For over a decade the government of the Netherlands had been protecting Arminius and his more radical followers from trial in the ecclesiastical courts. The government staunchly maintained that only a national synod could rule on the Arminian controversy but consistently refused to call a national synod to decide the question.

As a result of this tactic, by 1617 the Dutch church was on the verge of schism and the state was on the brink of civil war. Only a timely change of government averted these disasters and finally permitted the synod to meet.

Although the Arminian problem was tied intimately to the Dutch church and state, it was not exclusively a Dutch concern. Reformed theologians from Great Britain, France, Germany, and Switzerland had followed the development of the Arminian controversy with growing consternation.

Although communication between countries was slow in the seventeenth century, European theologians participated in a community of thought more than they do today. Latin was a common language in which they could all communicate. As students they also normally studied in several of the great European universities in the course of their education. Reformed scholars were attracted particularly to the most distinguished Reformed universities: Geneva, Heidelberg, Cambridge, and Leiden.

As a result of their international travels, theologians became personally acquainted with one another. Reformed theologians throughout Europe were kept informed of the issues in the United Provinces by personal conversations and correspondence. Several wrote treatises against the Arminians well before the Synod of Dort met.

Dutch theologians also realized that the impact of the Arminian controversy was not limited to the Netherlands. They realized the importance of an international Reformed consensus on the issues involved. Thus the Dutch invited theologians from the Reformed churches of Great Britain, France, and various areas of Germany and Switzerland to send delegates to the Synod of Dort.

All of the churches accepted the invitation, and, with the exception of France, the international delegates sat as full voting members of the synod. (While the French Reformed Church had appointed delegates to attend the synod, they never arrived at Dordrecht. King Louis XIII had declared that if the delegation left the country, members would not be allowed to return.)

Thus in a real sense this national synod was an international synod. The Synod of Dort functioned as an ecumenical Reformed council in a way that no Reformed gathering has before or since. The Canons of Dort therefore are not a Dutch production, but they represent an ecumenical consensus of the best minds in the whole Reformed community. The Canons of Dort are the least provincial or national of all Reformed doctrinal standards.

THE ISSUE AT THE SYNOD

One mistaken view of the Canons of Dort and the five points of Calvinism is that they deal with the theological periphery. Those who hold this notion prefer to stress doctrines held in common with other evangelicals. While they may admit that the Reformed distinctiveness of the Canons are valuable doctrinally, they do not see them as central and foundational.

This approach is not new. Arminians pursued this line of argument in the Netherlands by maintaining that their position did not deviate from the basics of Reformed doctrine. They claimed that their disagreements involved the-

Zacharius Ursinus

ological details of no more significance than the differences between infralapsarianism and supralapsarianism.

Before the synod was called, Franciscus Gomarus, one of the leading supralapsarian theologians, rejected this Arminian ploy. He declared that the issue between the Reformed and the Arminians was not some abstract detail of predestination. Rather, the heart of the Reformation was at issue—justification by faith in Christ alone. Reformed theologians, whether infralapsarian or supralapsarian, agreed with Gomarus in his analysis.

The Arminian doctrine of predestination held that God alone elects to eternal life those whom he foresees responding by faith to the gospel. Thus man's election becomes dependent on faith. Reformed theologians properly saw that this was a fundamental distortion of the Reformation's rediscovery of a biblical understanding of faith. Faith is a gift from God to the elect, not another good work, not a new legal condition for the new covenant. They rejected the Arminian attempt to make human cooperation again crucial to salvation. The Reformed theologians saw properly that the only way to protect justification by faith alone was to assert as clearly as possible that faith is completely a gift sovereignly given by God to those whom he has chosen.

Each head of doctrine in the canons therefore underscores, reinforces, and protects the foundational reality of Christianity: redemption is wholly of the Lord. The first head of doctrine stresses that faith is given to some on the basis of God's good pleasure alone, and not because of anything in the elect that makes them more worthy than others.

The second head of doctrine shows that Christ died to accomplish salvation completely for the elect, not to make salvation an abstract possibility.

The third and fourth heads of doctrine show that man is totally unable to help himself, being dead in sin and therefore totally dependent on the Holy Spirit to apply the benefits of Christ's death to the elect sovereignly, effectively, and fully.

The fifth head of doctrine comforts believers with the assurance that after the Holy Spirit has given the gift of faith to the elect, he preserves them so that unfailingly God's own are kept in the body of Christ throughout their lives.

COMPROMISE AT THE SYNOD

Another myth about the synod is that it expressed a particularly rigid and narrow statement of Calvinism. This attitude reflects a misunderstanding of the synod. When the orthodox delegates gathered at Dort, it soon became clear that there were significant differences among them.

While all were agreed that the Arminian theology was false and dangerous, they were not all agreed on how best to express the Reformed faith positively. Two particular areas of disagreement emerged: the doctrine of election and the extent of Christ's atonement.

On election, a large majority of the synod were infralapsarian while a prestigious minority were supralapsarian. On the extent of the atonement, a large majority were satisfied with the traditional formula—first used by Peter Lombard in the Middle Ages—that Christ's death was sufficient for all but efficient for the elect alone. Two groups dissented from this majority opinion: the first wanted to eliminate the category of sufficiency from the discussion, while the second wanted to stress and elaborate the notion of sufficiency.

The debate on the atoning death of Christ troubled the work of the synod in particular, and at one point some delegates threatened to leave. Theological wisdom and diplomatic necessity prevailed at the synod, however. During the discussions it became clear that the theological differences among the delegates were not on essentials and that a compromise formulation was possible. By a timely compromise the work of the synod was brought to fruition.

Today, compromise is often a despised word because too often theological compromise in recent decades has meant capitulation to gross theological error or heresy. But the compromise accomplished at Dort stands as a model for the life of the modern church. With rare sensitivity the Reformed theologians at Dort defended essential biblical truth while leaving room for legitimate theological differences among the orthodox. For example, the final statement of the canons allows for infralapsarian and supralapsarian interpretation. On the extent of the atonement, sufficiency and efficiency are taught, but the final nature of sufficiency is left open.

The canons, then, are not a rigid statement of monolithic Calvinist orthodoxy. Rather, the canons are a moderate, inclusive compromise drawing all Calvinists together around the essentials of the faith and preventing the movement from fragmenting over peripheral matters.

THE LANGUAGE OF THE CANONS

Delegates to the synod used two methods of presentation and discussion in their work. John Hales, an English observer of the synod, described them in his letters from Dort. On January 8, 1619, he noted with approval one discussion: "The order of discussing these arguments is by continued discourse after the manner of Latin sermons, or rather of divinity lectures, such as we have in our schools." Commenting on another discussion on January 18 of which he did not approve, he stated: "The manner of his discourse was oratorical, the same that he uses in his ser-

mons, not scholastical, and according to the fashion of disputation and the schools."

When the time came to write the canons, the synod had
to choose between these two methods of presentation: between the scholastic mode, that is, the technical form of a
theological school lecture, and a more popular manner, addressed to the church as a whole for its edification. Delegates decided that it would be most fruitful to frame the
canons so that they might be easily understood by and ed-
ifying to the churches. Hence the canons are not scholastic
but simple and straightforward in format.

To confirm this contention, one need only look at the first
head of doctrine as an example. Articles one through six
show precisely how election ought to be taught and how
this biblical doctrine ought to be discussed for strengthening the church. Following the biblical model, the canons begin with man's historic need of salvation, move on to God's
provision of Christ in history, and then relate God's effective provision of salvation to his eternal, sovereign, and free
will whereby some are elect and some are left in their sins.

THE RELEVANCE OF THE CANONS

The Synod of Dort met from November 1618 to May
1619. The long months of labor by the outstanding Reformed theologians of Europe produced a statement that
was widely hailed in the church as a brilliant expression of
biblical Christianity. The simple and popular language of
the canons spoke to the deepest needs of Christian people.

The canons called Christians to humility before God as
they realized their complete bondage to sin. The canons inspired gratitude for God's electing love and for the complete redemption accomplished in Christ and sovereignly
applied by the Holy Spirit. The canons spoke comfort to

Christian hearts, casting out fear and declaring God's love that would never let them go. The canons called the people of God to be liberated from morbid self-concern and to serve God in the world with love and joy.

The theology of the canons did not bludgeon the Reformed community into inaction but rather armed the Reformed church with the whole counsel of God. Strengthened with a confidence in God taught in the canons, Reformed Christians became the most dynamic and effective witnesses to Christ in Europe.

The church needs this vital biblical religion as much in the twenty-first century as in the seventeenth. The church needs the Reformation vision not merely to preserve a tradition. The church must be equipped to face the problems of today head-on. American Christianity is plagued not with too much knowledge of the Bible and theology but with too little.

Reformed Christians need to absorb the biblical insights of the canons afresh so that the truths presented will permeate their hearts and lives. When the truth of God empowers the church, people are redeemed and restored to the glory that God intended from the beginning.

17

CONFESSIONS AND TODAY'S CHURCH

Americans are forward-looking. Their interests are in the future and in progress. They tend to agree with Henry Ford's statement, "History is bunk."

Futurologists are fashionable serving as scientific prophets for the contemporary world. Technology fascinates us as it makes vast amounts of information available in a matter of seconds.

The great danger that this American tendency poses is that we will lose a proper working relationship with the wisdom of the past. We run the risk of being overwhelmed with the new and losing the venerable.

This character of American life affects Christian churches. Churches can get so excited about the latest fads derived from expert sociologists that they can fail to analyze those fads carefully. They can become so involved in preparing vision statements that they forget their confessions. We may fail to evaluate strategies and methodologies in a thoughtful theological and pastoral way.

The great danger of many American churches is that they will lose the center of faith. They risk getting caught up in something peripheral and missing the essential. For example, some seem to dedicate all their energies to evangelism but do not show that they know the gospel.

The great Reformed confessions contain for us the center that we need. They are the summary of biblical religion prepared by some of the church's best minds and most pious hearts. These confessions—especially the Westminster Confession of Faith, the Westminster Shorter and Larger Catechisms, the Heidelberg Catechism, the Belgic Confession, and the Canons of Dort—are full and rich. They must not be seen as an irrelevant or optional periphery to the life of the church. Even less should they be an ignored foundation. Rather, we must return to them again and again as the heart and core of the life and teaching of the church.

The apostle Paul in 2 Timothy 1:8–14 (NIV) wrote of the character of the message that he bore as apostle, herald, and teacher. He spoke of the Christian religion as "pattern" (v. 13), "deposit" (v. 14), and "sound teaching" (v. 13). While clearly recognizing that our Reformed confessions are not inspired, these concepts that Paul applied to his preaching can help us think about the meaning of our confessions.

Our confessions show us the pattern of biblical revelation. They are a pattern in the sense of an example or, even better, a standard. They show us something of the coherence and interconnectedness of God's truth. They help us to see the system of doctrine that God has revealed in his Word.

Many Christians know a variety of Bible stories or have a measure of insight into particular doctrines of the faith. But too often these stories or doctrines are left fragmented. The real meaning of the stories and doctrines may be missed because their relations to the whole of the Bible are misunderstood.

The pattern of the confessions reminds us that the truth of God is not only coherent but also broad and deep. The confessions remind us that God does not call us to an abbreviated or shrunken gospel.

We can see that clearly by the way in which Paul briefly summarizes his message in 2 Timothy 1. He gives no barebones gospel. Rather, he speaks of the gospel that brings the power of God for salvation and holy living. He speaks of this salvation as resting on the grace of God alone—a grace planned and purposed in eternity. This grace is brought to us by Jesus, who destroyed the death that was our life and who sovereignly and effectively has enlightened and enlivened us. This Jesus will protect and preserve his own until the day of his appearing. (Notice that in just five verses Paul speaks of or at least implies all five points of Calvinism!) His teaching is rich.

That same richness is in our confessional heritage. In a church that is shrinking because of starvation, we must bring out in fresh and clear ways the feast of truth that is ours in our confessions.

Our confessions are also a deposit. By deposit, Paul meant a property that had been entrusted from one to another to be guarded. It referred to a treasure that had to be valued and protected. Clearly the Scripture is such a deposit: God's Word given to us. But in a secondary sense our confessions are also our treasure.

They were written by men who were heroic preachers, wise theologians, and faithful martyrs. They were written in an age of unusual devotion, learning, and zeal. They have been defended for centuries by the best of our theologians.

Perhaps most remarkably our confessions have received an amazing level of support through the centuries. Often they were adopted in the first place by the unanimous action of church assemblies. Year by year they have been subscribed by the ministers and elders of Christ's church. When we think how hard it is today to get a church assembly to do anything unanimously, the support these confessions have received is a marvel.

Because such a remarkable consensus surrounds them, the confessions can and must serve as ballast for the church. They provide continuity and stability for the church as it sails through storms. They connect the church to its history and enable the church to share in the wisdom of past generations. They pull us together and help us overcome the corrosive individualism of our time. As we cherish and preserve our confessions, they will help protect us from the fads and novelties that beset the church today.

The Reformed confessions are also—like the gospel—sound teaching. Sound teaching is a recurring concern of Paul in the pastoral epistles. He mentions it in 1 Timothy 1:10; 6:3; 2 Timothy 1:13; 4:3; and Titus 1:9; 1:13; 2:1–2. By sound teaching he means healthy teaching, teaching that is not sick or poisonous. Paul knew that the church was often attacked by the evil one who sought to destroy the church with false teaching. In the face of such attacks the church needs healthy, useful teaching. Such teaching it has in its confessions.

Think for a moment about some of the problems the church faces. Christians today live in a radically relativistic culture. The confessions teach clearly about the unique revelation of God's Word found in the Bible as completely trustworthy, transcendent truth. Christians confront many cults. The confessions teach the Trinity and the person of Christ clearly. The church recognizes its evangelistic responsibility. The confessions summarize the doctrine of salvation. The confessions may not say all that needs to be said today to face all of these problems, but they do give us a solid foundation from which to build and minister.

Look more specifically at the helpful teaching found in some of the more neglected confessional statements. First, from the Canons of Dort: "Therefore all men are conceived in sin, and are by nature children of wrath, incapable of saving good, prone to evil, dead in sin, and in bondage thereto; and without the regenerating grace of the Holy Spirit, they are neither able nor willing to return to God, to reform the depravity of their nature, or to dispose themselves to reformation."[1]

This article reminds us that people are utterly lost in sin. They do not seek God. No clever methodology can move their wills. Only the Spirit of God can enliven them. So every method of evangelism and church growth must be examined to see if it takes seriously the complete deadness of the lost.

Or think of this article of the Canons of Dort:

As many as are called by the gospel are unfeignedly called. For God has most earnestly and truly declared in his Word what is acceptable to Him, namely that those who are called should come unto Him. He also seriously promises rest of soul and eternal life to all who come to Him and believe.[2]

This section of the canons guards all of us from any form of hyper-Calvinism that would make us passive in relation to our responsibility to make Christ known. We must preach Christ and passionately call people to believe in Christ. We must promise all who believe that they will certainly find salvation in him. What a wonderful encouragement!

Consider the Westminster Larger Catechism, question 109:

What are the sins forbidden in the second commandment? Answer: The sins forbidden in the second commandment are, all devising, counselling, commanding, using, and any wise approving, any religious worship not instituted by God himself; tolerating a false religion; the making any representation of God, or all or of any of the three persons, either inwardly in our mind, or outwardly in any kind of image or likeness of any creature whatsoever; all worshipping of it, or God in it or by it; the making of any representation of feigned deities, and all worship of them, or service belonging to them; all superstitious devices, corrupting the worship of God, adding to it, or taking from it, whether invented and taken up of ourselves, or received by tradition from others, though under the title of antiquity, custom, devotion, good intent, or any other pretense whatsoever; simony; sacrilege; all neglect, contempt, hindering, and opposing the worship and ordinances which God hath appointed.

This very long answer can be so daunting that a Christian may not even try to read or understand it. Yet it is not complex or difficult if it is read section by section. It speaks very much to the many questions about worship in the church today. It reminds us that God takes his worship seriously. It emphasizes that we must do in worship only what God commands—neither adding to it nor taking away from it. It warns that neither tradition nor sincerity justifies any practice in worship. Most importantly it should force all Reformed Christians as they talk about worship to go back to the Bible to see what it teaches.

The Reformed confessions are the pattern, deposit, and sound teaching for us. In order for them truly to function in that way we must become more familiar with them. We should commit ourselves to read them at least once a year. (It would be interesting to survey ministers and elders to see how often they read through their church's confessions.) We should read not only our own denomination's but also others'. We need to read them carefully. Where we do not understand them, we should study further. Where we may not agree, we should reexamine the issue—and especially ourselves! We should read them devotionally, letting their wisdom soak into us.

Our confessions will enrich us and fit us for service to Christ's church. They will help us experience the blessing expressed by Paul: "join with me in suffering for the gospel, by the power of God, who saved us and called us to a holy life. . . . What you heard from me, keep as the pattern of sound teaching, with faith and love in Christ Jesus. Guard the good deposit that was entrusted to you—guard it with the help of the Holy Spirit who lives in us" (2 Tim. 1:8–9, 13–14).

Notes

Chapter 1: Luther on Law and Gospel

1. Heiko A. Oberman, *Luther, Man between God and the Devil,* trans. Eileen Walliser-Schwartzbart (New Haven: Yale University, 1989).

2. Martin Luther, *Disputation against Scholastic Theology, 1517,* in *Luther's Works,* vol. 31, *Career of the Reformer* 1, ed. Harold J. Grimm and Helmut T. Lehman (Philadelphia: Fortress, 1957), 12.

3. Ibid., 9.

4. John Calvin and Jacopo Sadoleto, *A Reformation Debate: Sadoleto's Letter to the Genevans and Calvin's Reply,* ed. John C. Olin (New York: Harper, 1966), 32–33.

5. Martin Luther, "Preface to the Complete Edition of Luther's Latin Writings," in *Martin Luther: Selections from His Writings,* ed. John Dillenberger (New York: Anchor, 1961), 11.

6. Ibid.

7. Roland H. Bainton, *Here I Stand: A Life of Martin Luther* (New York: Abingdon-Cokesbury, 1950), 337.

8. Martin Luther, *The Freedom of a Christian,* in *Martin Luther: Selections from His Writings,* ed. John Dillenberger (New York: Anchor, 1961), 52.

9. Ibid., 53.

10. Martin Luther, *Lectures on Galatians 1–4, 1535*, in *Luther's Works*, vol. 26, ed. Jaroslav Pelikan (St. Louis: Concordia, 1995), 309–10.

11. Ibid., 5.

12. Ibid., 365.

13. Ibid., 313.

14. Martin Luther, *Table Talk*, in *Luther's Works*, vol. 54, ed. Theodore G. Tappert (Philadelphia: Fortress, 1967), 75.

15. Luther, *Lectures on Galatians*, 7.

16. Luther, *The Freedom of a Christian*, 52.

17. Cited in Robin A. Leaver, *Luther on Justification* (St. Louis: Concordia, 1975), 24.

18. Martin Luther, *Commentary on the Alleged Imperial Edict, 1531*, in *Luther's Works*, vol. 34, *Career of the Reformer 4*, ed. Helmut T. Lehman and Lewis W. Spitz (Philadelphia: Fortress, 1960), 91.

19. Martin Luther, *Lectures on Genesis 6–14, 1535*, in *Luther's Works*, vol. 2, ed. Jaroslav Pelikan (St. Louis: Concordia, 1995), 266–67.

20. Luther, *Lectures on Galatians*, 154–55.

21. Martin Luther, *The Disputation Concerning Justification, 1536*, in *Luther's Works*, vol. 34, *Career of the Reformer 4*, ed. Helmut T. Lehman and Lewis W. Spitz (Philadelphia: Fortress, 1960), 176.

22. Martin Luther, *On the Councils and the Church, 1539*, in *Luther's Works*, vol. 41, *Church and Ministry 3*, ed. Eric W. Gritsch (Philadelphia: Fortress, 1959), 166.

23. The Formula of Concord, in *The Book of Concord*, ed. T. Tappert (Philadelphia: Fortress, 1959), 480.

24. Martin Luther, *Large Catechism*, in *The Book of Concord*, 407.

25. Cited in Oberman, *Luther*, 129.

26. Martin Luther, *Sermon on the Sum of Christian Life, 1532*, in *Luther's Works*, vol. 51, *Sermons 1*, ed. John W. Doberstein (Philadelphia: Fortress, 1959), 284.

27. Martin Luther, *What Luther Says: An Anthology*, ed. Ewald M. Plass, 3 vols. (St. Louis: Concordia, 1959), 1128–29.

Chapter 2: Luther on the Family

1. Cited in Heiko Oberman, *Luther, Man between God and the Devil* (New Haven, Yale University, 1989), 272.

2. Martin Luther, *The Estate of Marriage, 1522,* in *Luther's Works,* vol. 45, *Christian in Society* 2, ed. Walther I. Brandt (Philadelphia: Fortress, 1962), 47.

3. Cited in Oberman, *Luther,* 272.

4. Cited in H. G. Haile, *Luther: An Experiment in Biography* (Garden City, N.Y.: Doubleday, 1980), 302.

5. Cited in Roland Bainton, *Here I Stand* (New York: Abingdon, 1950), 302.

6. Ibid., 301.

7. Ibid., 300.

8. Martin Luther, *The Estate of Marriage,* 46.

9. Cited in Bainton, *Here I Stand,* 293.

10. Cited in ibid., 304.

11. Luther, *The Estate of Marriage,* 40–41.

Chapter 3: The Forgotten 97 Theses

1. Martin Luther, *Disputation against Scholastic Theology, 1517,* in *Luther's Works,* vol. 31, *Career of the Reformer* 1, ed. Harold J. Grimm and Helmut T. Lehman (Philadelphia: Fortress, 1957), 9–16.

Chapter 4: The Celebrated 95 Theses

1. Martin Luther, *Ninety-five Theses,* in *Luther's Works,* vol. 31, *Career of the Reformer* 1, ed. Harold J. Grimm and Helmut T. Lehman (Philadelphia: Fortress, 1957). Also *Martin Luther's Ninety-Five Theses,* ed. Stephen J. Nichols (Phillipsburg, N.J.: P&R, 2002).

Chapter 5: The Power of the Gospel

1. Martin Luther, "The Last Sermon, Preached in Eisleben, 1546," in *Luther's Works,* vol. 51, *Sermons* 1, ed. John W. Doberstein (Philadelphia: Fortress, 1959), 383–92.

Chapter 6: The Forgotten Reformer

1. Philip Melanchthon, *Loci Communes, 1543,* trans. J. A. O. Preus (St. Louis: Concordia, 1992).

2. Clyde Leonard Manschreck, *Melanchthon, the Quiet Reformer* (New York: Abingdon, 1958).

Chapter 7: Melanchthon at Five Hundred

1. Philip Melanchthon, *Loci Communes, 1543,* trans. J. A. O. Preus (St. Louis: Concordia, 1992), 84.

2. Philip Melanchthon, *Commentary on Romans,* trans. Fred Kramer (St. Louis: Concordia, 1992), 18.

3. Melanchthon, *Loci Communes,* 97.

4. The Augsburg Confession, art. 20.

5. Melanchthon, *Loci Communes,* 92.

6. Melanchthon, *Commentary on Romans,* 70.

7. Ibid., 70–71.

8. Ibid., 29–30.

9. The Augsburg Confession, art. 20.

10. Melanchthon, *Loci Communes,* 93.

11. Melanchthon, *Commentary on Romans,* 28.

Chapter 8: Calvin the Churchman

1. John Calvin to William Farel, 1541, in *Selected Works of John Calvin: Tracts and Letters,* ed. Henry Beveridge and Jules Bonnet, 7 vols. (Grand Rapids, Mich.: Baker, 1983), 4:244.

2. John Calvin to William Farel, 1541, in *Selected Works of John Calvin,* 4:260.

3. John Calvin to Thomas Cranmer, 1552, in *Selected Works of John Calvin,* 5:347–48.

4. John Calvin to William Farel, 1541, in *Selected Works of John Calvin,* 4:284.

5. John Calvin to Oswald Myconius, in *Selected Works of John Calvin,* 4:316.

6. John Calvin to William Farel, 1541, in *Selected Works of John Calvin,* 4:285.

7. John Calvin to William Farel, in *Selected Works of John Calvin,* 4:263.

8. Ibid.

9. John Calvin to William Farel, in *Selected Works of John Calvin,* 4:261.

10. John Calvin to William Farel, in *Selected Works of John Calvin,* 4:263.

Chapter 9: Calvin on Church Unity

1. John Calvin, *Commentary on the Book of Psalms,* 5 vols. (Grand Rapids, Mich.: Baker, 1979), 1:189.

2. Ibid., 5:293–94.

3. Ibid., 5:164–65.

4. Ibid., 1:204–5.

5. Ibid., 5:166.

Chapter 10: A Response to Trent

1. *Canons and Decrees of the Council of Trent: Original Text with English Translation,* trans. H. J. Schroeder (London: Herder, 1941). See, for example, session 6, chaps. 1 and 5.

2. Ibid., session 6, chaps. 8 and 11.

3. Ibid., session 6, chaps. 7 and 16.

4. Ibid., session 6, chap. 7.

5. Ibid., session 6, chap. 11.

6. Ibid., session 6, chaps. 9, 12, and 13.

7. John Calvin, *Acts of the Council of Trent: With the Antidote,* ed. and trans. Henry Beveridge (1851), in *Selected Works of John Calvin: Tracts and Letters,* ed. Henry Beveridge and Jules Bonnet, 7 vols. (Grand Rapids, Mich.: Baker, 1983), 3:17–188.

8. Ibid., 3:113.

9. Ibid., 3:125.

10. Ibid., 3:115.

11. Ibid., 3:116.

12. Ibid., 3:134.

13. Ibid., 3:125.

14. Ibid., 3:135.

15. Ibid., 3:136.

Chapter 11: A Response to Bolsec

1. John Calvin, *Selected Works of John Calvin: Tracts and Letters,* ed. Henry Beveridge and Jules Bonnet, 7 vols. (Grand Rapids, Mich.: Baker, 1983), 5:323.

2. John Calvin, *Institutes of the Christian Religion,* ed. John T. McNeill, trans. Ford Lewis Battles, 2 vols., Library of Christian Classics (Philadelphia: Westminster, 1960), 1.21.1.

3. Ibid., 1.22.10.

4. Ibid., 1.21.1.

5. Ibid.

6. T. H. L. Parker, *John Calvin: A Biography* (Philadelphia: Westminster, 1975), 113.

7. John Calvin to Heinrich Bullinger, 15 October 1551, in *Selected Works of John Calvin,* 5:321–22.

8. Ibid., 5:320–21.

9. John Calvin to Heinrich Bullinger, March 1552, in *Selected Works of John Calvin,* 5:342ff.

10. In *Selected Works of John Calvin,* 5:323.

11. Ibid., 5:324.

12. Ibid.

13. Calvin to Bullinger, March 1552, in *Selected Works of John Calvin,* 5:344.

14. John Calvin to Heinrich Bullinger, January 1553, in *Selected Works of John Calvin,* 5:332.

15. Ibid., 5:332–33.

16. Ibid., 5:333.

17. Ibid.

18. Ibid.

19. Ibid., 5:334.

20. John Calvin to William Farel, January 1553, in *Selected Works of John Calvin,* 5:335.

21. Ibid., 5:336.

22. Ibid.

23. Ibid.

24. John Calvin, *Concerning the Eternal Predestination of God,* trans. J. K. S. Reid (London: James Clarke, 1961), 56–58.

Chapter 14: An International Reformer

1. Peter Martyr, *The Life, Early Letters, and Eucharistic Writings of Peter Martyr*, ed. Joseph C. McLelland and G. E. Duffield (n.p.: Sutton Courtney, 1989), 51.

Chapter 15, A Catechism from Heidelberg

1. Zacharias Ursinus, *The Commentary of Dr. Zacharias Ursinus on the Heidelberg Catechism*, trans. George W. Williard (Phillipsburg, N.J.: P&R, 1985).

Chapter 17, Confessions and Today's Church

1. Canons of Dort, heads of doctrine 3–4, art. 3.
2. Ibid., heads of doctrine 3–4, art. 8.

INDEX OF PERSONS

W. ROBERT GODFREY (Ph.D., Stanford University) is professor of church history and president at Westminster Theological Seminary in California. He is a minister of the United Reformed Churches, and is a contributing editor of The Outlook. Godfrey coedited Theonomy: A Reformed Critique, contributed to John Calvin: His Influence in the Western World and several other volumes, and has written numerous articles. He has been a speaker at numerous conferences, including the Lausanne Committee for World Evangelization, the Philadelphia Conference on Reformed Theology, and Ligonier Ministries.